Kathleen Collins

Visionaries: Thinking Through Female Filmmakers
Series Editors Lucy Bolton and Richard Rushton

Titles in the series include:

The Cinema of Marguerite Duras: Feminine Subjectivity and Sensoriality
Michelle Royer

Ana Kokkinos: An Oeuvre of Outsiders
Kelly McWilliam

Kathleen Collins: The Black Essai Film
Geetha Ramanathan

Habiba Djahnine: Memory Bearer
Sheila Petty

edinburghuniversitypress.com/series/vision

Kathleen Collins

The Black Essai Film

Geetha Ramanathan

EDINBURGH
University Press

For Kehan DeSousa

Edinburgh University Press is one of the leading university presses in the UK. We publish academic books and journals in our selected subject areas across the humanities and social sciences, combining cutting-edge scholarship with high editorial and production values to produce academic works of lasting importance. For more information visit our website: edinburghuniversitypress.com

We are committed to making research available to a wide audience and are pleased to be publishing Platinum Open Access editions of the ebooks in this series.

© Geetha Ramanathan, 2020, under a Creative Commons Attribution-NonCommercial licence

Edinburgh University Press Ltd
The Tun—Holyrood Road
12(2f) Jackson's Entry
Edinburgh EH8 8PJ

Typeset in 12/14 Arno and Myriad by
IDSUK (DataConnection) Ltd

A CIP record for this book is available from the British Library

ISBN 978 1 4744 4068 4 (hardback)
ISBN 978 1 4744 4070 7 (webready PDF)
ISBN 978 1 4744 4069 1 (paperback)
ISBN 978 1 4744 4071 4 (epub)

The right of Geetha Ramanathan to be identified as the author of this work has been asserted in accordance with the Copyright, Designs and Patents Act 1988, and the Copyright and Related Rights Regulations 2003 (SI No. 2498).

Contents

List of figures   vi
Acknowledgments   vii

Introduction   1
1. The New York Black Independents   13
2. The black essai film   31
3. Ambiguities of auteurship   51
4. The magical marvelous modern   83
5. Sacred doubles   100
6. Film across drama and art   117
7. Black feminist culture and black masculinity   132

Afterword   150

Bibliography   152
Filmography   161
Index   164

Figures

1.1	*Ganja and Hess*: Inhabiting the landscape	16
2.1	*Cruz Brothers*: The brothers in Miss Malloy's house	39
2.2	*Losing Ground*: Playing the role of Frankie	48
2.3	*Carmen Jones*: "I could have been another Dorothy Dandridge." Sara in *Losing Ground*	48
2.4	*Carmen Jones*: Violence against women	49
3.1	*Cruz Brothers*: The ethnographer	61
3.2	*Cruz Brothers*: The figure of fate?	62
3.3	*Losing Ground*: "Form, color, light"	71
3.4	*Losing Ground*: "Don't you take your dick out like it was artistic like it's some goddamn paintbrush"	73
3.5	*Losing Ground*: Male artist/auteur	75
4.1	*Cruz Brothers*: Miss Malloy greets the brothers	92
4.2	*Cruz Brothers*: Nostalgia or desire?	96
5.1	*Losing Ground*: Sara and Duke in the metafilm	111
5.2	*Losing Ground*: Johnny betrays Frankie	112
6.1	*Losing Ground*: The second screen	119
6.2	*Losing Ground*: Tableau vivant	124

Acknowledgments

I am deeply grateful to the Schomburg Center for Research in Black Culture in allowing me access to the material of Kathleen Collins. Nina Lorez Collins was extremely generous in allowing me to work with her mother, Kathleen Collins's, unpublished plays, and other writings. Thank you.

The College of Arts and Humanities at West Chester University provided me with a RACA grant to do the research for this book. Thanks are particularly due to Dr. Hyoejin Yoon who facilitated the process.

My gratitude to Professor James Trotman, Founding Director of the Douglass Institute for his expansive vision of African American literature and culture.

Warm thanks to Lucy Bolton and Richard Rushton for their careful reading of the typescript.

I deeply appreciate the assistance of Joe Watts of the Digital Media Centre for his work on the clips in this book. Thanks as usual to Dana, Amanda, Neil, and Jenn at FH Green Library.

I am grateful to the Edinburgh University Press production team for their diligence, particularly Eliza Wright.

On a more personal note, I would like to thank Mona Fayad, who has been extremely supportive. Thanks also to Neus Bonet Farran who accompanied me on yet another research trip, and Anil for hospitality. And lastly, Vek for his enthusiasm for the project, and Dhario for many conversations on black film.

Introduction

This book makes the case that Kathleen Collins decisively redefined the parameters of African American film with *The Cruz Brothers and Miss Malloy* and *Losing Ground*. Collins's presentation of black interiority effectively inserts film as a "positive scene of instruction" for African Americans, correcting the pejorative values attached to African American film as the "negative scene of instruction" (Wallace 1993b: 212). As a cultural tool, film consistently appears unassailable for African Americans. Collins comments on the persistence of Hollywood definitions of African Americans on the cultural imaginary:

> Film is the biggest, most powerful and most potent mythology. And we have not reflected on the possibility of our being able to use this mythology ... The Gods and Goddesses of America are film stars. This is the Greek mythology of America and we don't know where we fit in this mythology. How can we take a camera in our hands and speak of this sacred myth of film and Hollywood when we would damage this mythology? (Franklin 1980)

In decisively inserting black/minority authority in her films, Collins intervenes in this celluloid cult of a quasi-divine white nation where black/minority subjects are invisible or diminished in scale. Her films *The Cruz Brothers and Miss Malloy* (1980) and *Losing Ground* (1982) offer a world view sharply at odds with received Hollywood mythologies on African Americans.

Conventions of blackface in the cinema of attractions and early silent film render the presence of black subjects on screen hypothetical, ultimately fantasmatic. Black presence was simultaneously obviated, and referenced metonymically as the grotesque (Danow 1995). Wallace's comment about the extremely distraught relationship between blackness and visuality/visibility persists in other visual formats, even the strictly mimetic such as CCTV that capitalize on a dialectic of white invisibility and black visibility to narrativize blackness as "socially undesirable" (Marriot 2007: xiv). White invisibility, black visibility but black absence has persisted since early silent film, *The Birth of a Nation* (dir. Griffith, 1915) functioning as a model.

African American film criticism has established that *The Birth of a Nation* constructed a cinematic world where black subjects had forfeited the right to exist except as appendages to white superiors, what Manthia Diawara identifies as "the ban on Blacks participating in bourgeois humanism on Hollywood screens" (1993: 4–5). Further, by inscribing an unthinking racial binary, the film excluded black subjects from national belonging, rendering them the abject of white citizens. *The Birth of a Nation* was not the only repository of such imagery; earlier silent films had purveyed these images, although it is important to note that many films were ambivalent about codings of racial superiority (Stewart 2005: 1–19). The film's sophisticated narrative and aesthetic polish exerted disproportionate influence on cinema history, and on the public imaginary. The drama is played out in the very title of the film in the presumed contrast between the Klansmen's defense of the nation as embodied by the virtue of the white "lady" and the villainous black buck who rends the ideals of the "new" nation. The white woman is synecdochic of the white nation; defending her establishes the purity and whiteness of the nation. The over-sexed black buck with the whites of his teeth gleaming, produced by the stock that accentuated the blackface features of the white actor playing the role, would remain a staple of the national imaginary. Its continued sway over the cultural iconography of African Americans is eloquently parodied in

Spike Lee's 2018 *BlacKkKlansman* where he shows a chapter of the Klansmen watching the more infamous clips of the movie after the investiture of the latest Klansman. The film functions as an unholy palimpsest to the moment in the 1970s when the film is set, and to contemporary white nationalist marches.

The Birth of a Nation established four major archetypes that dominated the screen, and as late as the 1990s, students of African American film classes could identify them in shows in black television networks and mainstream film: for men, the coon and the buck; for women, the Jezebels and the mammies. "Bourgeois humanism" is further rendered impossible by the Motion Picture Production Code, or "Hays Code" (1930), that the Motion Picture Association used to censor itself to forestall state interference with the content of the films. The Code explicitly forbade any story involving miscegenation and/or imaging of interracial romance. Thus, black subjects alone—this did not include people of Latin American origin—were barred from enjoying the magic of the movies, the love story.

Blackface with respect to women continues even after the emergence of sound film that effectively allowed black subjects historical presence as distinct from the ghosted absent menace that primitive or silent film enjoined. During the sound era the idea of black women as part of the fabric of nation remains largely unacceptable. Mark Reid sums this up pithily in his comment about films from the 1930s including the canonical *Imitation of Life* (dir. Stahl, 1934):

> In one brushstroke these films paint interracial landscapes in varying racial tones and with another brushstroke hide cultural difference behind the pale mask of white actresses. These blackface romances permitted mainstream film audiences to safely consume the black heroine's corporal image without fear of transgressing codes that forbid miscegenation. Honoring these codes insured [sic] the screening of most of these films in the South where racial segregation condemned racial border crossings of all kinds. (Reid 2005: 80)

Thus, in a curious circumvention of the Hays Code of 1930 whereby black Americans were not to be seen in romantic relationships with european americans,[1] these films continued to purvey the Hegelian master–slave dialectic, reinforcing the cinematic national imaginary. Reid brings this point into play to argue that these tropes are being reiterated in US films as late as the 1990s when both of Collins's films had already been released. Comedies such as *White Men Can't Jump* (dir. Shelton, 1992) and *Made in America* (dir. Benjamin, 1993) do not really move away from the minstrel tradition in film (Reid 2005: 79).

The philosophical tone of Collins's films in the early 1980s, at a time when fairly tiresome tropes on race were being exercised, not unsurprisingly, resulted in a mixed reception, suggesting perhaps that audiences had not really been prepared for the kind of films she, along with other independent black filmmakers, had set out to make (Horak 2015; Stallings 2015). Collins's film had been released in the independent circuit—the Museum of Modern Art had screened *Losing Ground* as part of its Cineprobe series in 1983[2]—but did not secure the kind of commercial release that Lee's *Do the Right Thing* (1989) had. Critical emphasis on sociological representation, and a unitary black identity politics in evaluating African American film skewed the reception of Collins's films. Critics are beginning to recognize black female auteurial presence in film if only in the alternative sector, suggesting that Kathleen Collins along with Alile Sharon Larkin "have been revered as outstanding and influential independent voices" (Donalson 2003: 6). A more recent reading of her work that places her outside the identity politics of the LA School of independents is accurate (Beverly 2012). That black film could have value as art was a minority perspective, the representational load being the only criterion. One critic's polemic, as recently as 2016, urging that black film be included in black visual culture, speaks to the continued dominance of exclusively sociological values in discussing African American film (Harris 2016). Of course, there were a group of black women filmmakers who, like Collins, attended to themes that were different from what mainstream cinema produced, independent filmmakers, such as Zeinabu irene Davis and Camille Billops, among others. However, their focus on the "ancestral archive," a hearkening back to African traditions and heritage as part of the search for identity, speaks only partly to Collins's work (Ryan 2005). It is in this context that Reid correctly acknowledges Collins's contribution. Under the heading "The Womanist Film and the Black Professional," he maintains that "*Losing Ground* marks the first appearance of a black professional woman as protagonist in black independent films, and it is one of a very few portrayals of developing feminist consciousness in a black professional woman in any feature-length film" (Reid 2005: 121).

With the trope of the artist/intellectual/professional woman, Collins allows black female characters access to what Diawara calls "bourgeois humanism" (1993: 4). Sara, the lead character in *Losing Ground*, is, in other words, allowed to think and worry about matters not exclusively connected with race, such as intellectual creativity, passion, pleasure, art, work. Collins viewed women's creativity as an unpredictable and potentially threatening force; she was deeply aware of how dangerous a woman's intellect could be to her settling comfortably in her role as a woman in society. Interestingly, she identifies this belief as feminist:

> But if there is any way in which women tend to be self-destructive it is in that area of creativity where they actually feel their own power and can't either acknowledge it or go into it with as much ...
> They can't go to the end of it. They get scared and they retreat into illness or into having too many babies or destructive love affairs with men who run them ragged. Somewhere or other, they detour out of a respect for their own creativity. (Nicholson 1988/9: 9)

In choosing topics such as female creativity and authority, Collins was stepping into new territory even as the cultural wars on black authenticity were raging. Were critiques, particularly feminist critiques, sufficiently black, or were they hostile to authentic blackness? In exploring a black female's critical view of the artistic and intellectual black community, Collins was forced to counter constructions of blackness and of black femininity. The policing of what black art should be is also noted by a "shocked" Nicholson. *Losing Ground*, screened at Spelman College, a historically black university in Atlanta, Georgia, elicited this response from one man who told Collins that she was a "race traitor." That she "hewed to no party line," but sought out moral subtlety, also discomfited an unnamed, well-known filmmaker who said, "he did not like *Losing Ground* because it was a negative portrait of a black marriage" (Nicholson 1988/9: 7). A 2017 *New York Amsterdam News* report entitled "Visionary Filmmaker Kathleen Collins Featured" is a measure of how welcome her ideas are now, almost thirty-five years down the road: "It [*Losing Ground*] was never released widely, in part because at the time, and [sic] it was not racially reflective of the Black Experience" (Matthews 2017). Whose Black Experience?

That Collins also made a film about another minority group, Puerto Ricans living in New York, was equally incomprehensible. She reports that while making *The Cruz Brothers and Miss Malloy* she was repeatedly asked why she wanted to make a movie about "some Puerto Ricans and some dying Irish lady" (Nicholson 1988/9: 13). The quirky dance between the Puerto Rican boys and the Irish woman in *Cruz Brothers* speaks of existential choices that bypass identity politics. The stakes were high for Collins, who had explored the magical expansion of boundaries in the 1960s during her participation in the Freedom Riders. The Civil Rights Movement of the 60s, with its promise of the summer of love, peace and freedom for all, and specifically the attack against Jim Crow, could be expected to be an epistemic breach of a historic pattern of nullifying and segregating black masculinity and femininity from the larger culture.

In 1961 the Congress of Racial Equality called for black and white students to ride in buses together from the northeast of the United States to New Orleans to participate in the seventh anniversary of the decision on *Brown vs. Board of Education* that ordered the integration of public schools. In the South, however, white-only waiting rooms were the norm; Jim Crow was still king, and blacks were never permitted to sit in the front of the bus; consequently, seating black and white students together was regarded as a bold, if not radical move towards integration. Middle-class college students, black and white, male and female, were trained by the Congress in techniques of non-violent protest. That Martin Luther King Jr. chose not to join the Freedom Riders caused one of the first rifts in the Civil Rights Movement. The 1960 Supreme Court ruling that segregation of black people in buses was against the law spurred the students who were largely bourgeois and who were appalled that there were other Americans who were still being subject to Jim Crow despite the ruling. For the black bourgeoisie it was a challenge that leaves lasting psychic tremors. Kathleen Collins, the only black student in her classes at the elite Skidmore College, its student body almost all white, went South too, and as a nineteen-year-old was imprisoned briefly in an Albany cell, came back to her hometown of Jersey City in New Jersey, and reported on the struggle to end segregation, expressing hope.[3] A collection of short stories entitled *Whatever Happened to Interracial Love?* reflects on "race" as defined by this moment, suggesting that if young european americans were startled by the lived realities of race in the South, so were privileged African Americans living in the North. Collins's family had been in the States since the *Mayfair*. The divestiture of that kind of "Negro" privilege would be, in most cases, psychologically challenging, particularly the sense that many light-skinned elite blacks had been living an unreality, ever attempting to become "lighter" and to be the "first" black in different fields of endeavor including politics and education. Collins explores these scars on racial and gender identities in her fiction and her plays. One thread runs through her work on these themes, whether visible or invisible, of the notionality of race, of how an abstract, distant construct prevents black women and men from experiencing their humanity fully; at the fullest moment, blackness or non-blackness threatens to drain the joy, leaving only the void.

In place of identifying exclusively as black, Collins identified as black *and* ... She preferred the term minority, in the most expansive sense possible (Rhinehart 2016). In both her films, the central figures are characters, defined as minorities, who are invested in recording their stories, aware of trying to both ground themselves and lose themselves. Sara of *Losing Ground* grapples with the path to otherworldly ecstasy—mystical, erotic, mystical and erotic (Ramanathan 2006; Stallings 2011). Sara's framework is comparative and philosophical as she seeks to expand the traditional boundaries of western metaphysics. The trope of the book in African American literature, central to the emphasis on literacy and the intellect, functions as a mnemonic device in the film. A relatively unusual motif, if powerful, in both African American and women's film, it occurs in Germaine Dulac's *The Smiling Madame Beudet* (1923) when Mme. Beudet, a latter-day Mme. Bovary figure, reads Baudelaire and becomes aware of her own desire. Sara, on the other hand, suffers because of being an intellectual: aside from her students who admire her, the culture constantly admonishes her for being bookish and apprehending life through books. While it is not surprising for an intellectual to attempt to understand the world through letters, what might be admirable in other groups makes of Sara an oddity—a black woman intellectual.

Victor in *The Cruz Brothers* is presented as an ethnographer in the making, a character comparable to the young black photographer in Lee's *Joe's Bed-Stuy Barbershop* (1983), but unlike him, Victor is isolated and struggling to make larger generalizations about his community. Victor is the oldest of three brothers. Their father, shot in a bank robbery gone awry, appears only to Victor. The film itself is based on a short story written by Henry Roth, who was a colleague of Collins in the City College of New York.

Unlike some of her contemporaries, such as Spike Lee and Charles Burnett, Collins did not go to film school to learn filmmaking but had academic credentials in film theory and had done work towards a doctorate in French cinema. As a master's student of French literature, she went to Paris and studied at the Middlebury College at the Sorbonne where she took a course in

French literature and film that captivated her; the art of adapting stories to film or finding the language to narrate the story in film was to be an abiding interest (Collins 1984a). She translated for *Cahiers du cinema* and did a monograph for Editions du Seuil entitled *Cinéma et Racisme* in 1969.[4] She notes that she did not really care for Hollywood but was an avid reader. The literary influence—reading and writing—features prominently in her films (Klotman [1982] 2015).

In all, by 1988, Collins had written four screenplays. As early as 1971, she had written the script of "Women, Sisters, and Friends" and had gone around the country trying to find funding but was repeatedly told that although the script was a "wonderful idea," she should find someone else to direct and produce it. She found the path to the director's chair well and truly blocked. Collins is matter of fact about it: "Nobody would give any money to a black woman to direct a film" (Nicholson 1988/9: 10). *The New Yorker*'s Richard Brody was to rave about the script as the best film that no one would be able to stream on Netflix in February 2019 (Brody 2019). While not having access to film direction in the 1970s, Collins did become among the first in the country to start teaching film, which was newly emerging as a respectable field of study in the US. From 1974, she taught directing and screen writing in City College of New York (Nicholson 1988/9: 10). By that time, she had had considerable hands-on experience in editing, which she regarded as nothing short of "magical" (Klotman [1982] 2015). She had worked on editing several films, including Ossie Davis's *Cotton Comes to Harlem* (1970), for which she was not credited. A skilled editor, she won first prize for editing at the Cannes Film Festival 1970 for a short, *Stock Exchange Transplant* (dir. Collins, 1970), and first prize for editing the feature film *Touching Ground*, also directed by Douglas Collins, at the Chicago Film Festival, also in 1970.[5]

Difficult as it is for most independent filmmakers to find funding for their projects, all of them struggling for the same limited funds, it is even more difficult for African American filmmakers, and almost miraculous for an African American woman who wants to make a feature-length film. As Michelle Parkerson put it in a tribute issue of *Black Film Review*, "She [Collins] was among the first generation of Black female directors breaching the 'inner sanctum' of feature film production" (1988/9: 5).

Collins's universalist philosophy is apparent in her exploration of the characters in *Cruz Brothers* and *Losing Ground*. How important is identity politics to black and minority subjects in New York City, its suburbs, and the US in the 1980s? Collins throws these questions to her characters through the action of the film, bringing her formidable theatrical experience to bear in setting up situations, and in developing them.

Overview

The approach of this book is comparative, historical, and formalistic in its attention to cinematic detail. While offering full-length interpretations of the film, I embed the films in the larger discussion on otherness, visuality in relationship to aurality and to black female identity, the role of art in life and life in art, and the place of philosophy in art and film.

The book's core argument is that Collins probes areas of fundamental human existence in highly explosive social and political confrontations but offers resolutions, or approaches, that forward her desire that everyone find a way to their story. And in this endeavor, her films reveal the interiority and narrate the stories of those who in their passionate search had been silenced because they were thought to have no ideas.

Through the chapters, the book makes connections between Collins and other feminist filmmakers, particularly in terms of cinematic strategies, to further secure Collins in the canon of world feminist film, and to consolidate her place in the African American film tradition (Ramanathan 2006: 141–68). Collins's contributions to the New York Black Independents, along with the importance of the New York film movement, enriches African American film history, as it does the history of women filmmakers and that of independent filmmakers.

Chapter 1 traces the diverse genres of the black independent movement, draws out a genealogy of black filmmakers, and identifies connections across script writers, camera persons, directors, and actors. Featuring a comparative analysis of both the Los Angeles School and the New York School, the chapter seeks to draw out the specificity of the philosophy of art and race that Collins explores.

Chapter 2 contextualizes ideas of contemporary philosophers and writers on the cosmopolitan and universalist to suggest some ways in which to locate and identify Collins's visionary aspects as seen in the films. Whether it is a Cruz brother who tells his story through the visions he has of his father, or the painter who does it through abstract art, Collins introduces and develops a new genre of African American film: the black essai film.

Chapter 3 returns to a topic of perennial fascination for film scholars, and of more immediate urgency for African American film: auteurship. For both european and euro-american women it has been difficult to claim the exalted title of auteur, reserved for the likes of a Truffaut or a Hitchcock. Collins would appear to be ambivalent about the status of the auteur, or the grand creator with his/her vision of the film. Both her films question whether the creator is more important than the created, whether the architect is more central than the journeywoman/man, seriously deconstructing the authority of the auteur over her text. Yet, even as an example of the cancellation of auteurial control, her world view as translated by the techniques of filmmaking leaves no doubt as to the legitimacy of her place in film history as an auteur with a distinctive vision realized through a very specific visual and auditory aesthetic.

In the next three chapters, I seek to identify the moment that the character in the diegesis moves from her/his space and occupies the space of the other. I discuss the use of modernist aesthetics and magical realism in articulating these shifts. Is either mode more useful to moving beyond the limited? How does this change enhance individual authenticity? How is this authenticity implicated in universalism? How does it help one identify one's story? How does Collins shift the notion of the "minor" character? How does this aesthetic construct affect our views of the dominant majority and the minority? With a view to being specific about the strategies Collins uses to convey her ideas, I analyze the films in detail with respect to visuality and the auditory in these readings of as many as three sequences from each film. In part, the analysis is formalist and semiotic. The purpose of these chapters is to show the intricate connections between narrative, philosophy of race, and visuality as played out in the films. I conclude that Collins's inter-arts approach, situating film and visuality as one of the components of a larger African American/African American feminist cultural production, finally allows cinema to serve as "the positive scene of instruction" for African American culture (Wallace 1993b: 212).

The final chapter discusses the themes and techniques of some of Collins's published and unpublished writings to indicate that her vision of black masculinity and black femininity was informed by an awareness of how black women artists consistently resist racial bracketings to expand universal understandings

Notes

1 I use 'european american', 'european' and 'euro-american' lower case throughout to counter the privileging of european american women in feminist discourse, and the equation of women as a universal category with european american women.
2 MOMA would later screen *Losing Ground* in October 2017.
3 See <http://kathleencollins.org/about> (last accessed June 29, 2019).
4 Although *Cinéma et Racisme* is mentioned in Collins's curriculum vitae in archival material at the Schomburg Center for Research in Black Culture in New York, I have not been able to locate either the translation or the monograph. Editions du Seuil's reproduction department states that it does not have this title.
5 Listed in Collins's curriculum vitae in archival material in the Schomburg Center for Research in Black Culture. Not related to Kathleen Collins.

1

The New York Black Independents

The recent history of African American film studies has been devoted to the twin goals of critiquing dominant representations and presenting the work of independent black filmmakers. Black independent filmmaking has a long history stretching back to the silent era when "race" films were popular. It is salutary to note that the work of independent filmmakers, including that of pioneering silent movie director, Oscar Micheaux, who had produced and exhibited a huge corpus, did not begin to receive scholarly attention until the 1970s. Early responses found Micheaux's films wanting by Hollywood studio standards (Bogle 1973). The 80s and 90s challenged this view of Micheaux, and "race films," arguing that the techniques used presented rhetorical statements relevant to African American audiences (Cripps 1993; Gaines 1993; Bowser et al. 2001). Interest in these films was widespread among these audiences, who were avid moviegoers but were confined to specific areas of the movie theatre. However, between 1910 and 1925 they could avail of the 425 black-owned theatres that were indicative of African American investment in the motion picture business (Streible 1993). Interest in recording the history of black participation in the industry is unflagging, and film scholars have been sustained in their efforts to recover the history of black independent filmmaking, particularly to retrieve and restore the films of the silent era. There were about 125 independent companies producing hundreds of films in the hope of "[countering] prevailing caricatures of African-Americans on film" (Pearl Bowser qtd in Reed [1980] 2018). The coming of sound slowly put these companies out of business, but materials pertaining to their history, insofar as they have come to light, have been preserved by archivist Pearl Bowser in a collection called "African Diaspora Images."

While there are significant aesthetic differences in approach between black independent filmmakers of the earlier part of the century and the Los Angeles School in the 1960s, the imperative to challenge illusionistic Hollywood projections of black subjects remains a constant. The work of Kathleen Collins belongs to this capacious genre, more specifically to the group called New York Black Independents. Not only did Collins play a central role in this group in the 1970s, she also helped shape its aesthetic vision.

When asked if she considered herself a black filmmaker, Collins said that she thought of herself as a person who had an instinctive understanding of what it meant to belong to a minority (Franklin 1981).[1] As with many black independent filmmakers, the significance of Kathleen Collins's work for African American, world, and feminist film has only recently been recognized by the larger public. Programmed by Michelle Materre and Jake Perlin, the Lincoln Center's film screenings "Tell It Like It Is: Black Independents in New York, 1968–1986" brought her work to a wider audience. Among the films that were shown at the retrospective were Spike Lee's *She's Gotta Have It* (1986), Charles Lane's *Sidewalk Stories* (1989), and an impressive series of documentaries, including *Will* (dir. Maple, 1981) and *I Remember Harlem* (dir. Miles, 1981). Collins's *Losing Ground* headlined the series.

Since then, the New York Black Independents have also received significant scholarly attention as part of a focused academic venture "toward recovery as a prioritized practice" (Forster 2015: 64). In a discussion on the larger implications of such research, Forster (2015) notes that the continued investment of black audiences in sociologically verifiable representations might tempt audiences to see past the repertoires of performance in buried material to locate true, or singular, records of a black time past. He credits the curators of the series with offering a wide enough range of films to counteract notions of an unmediated back access to a definitive black past. The inclusion of diverse genres helped to draw attention to the role that genre and performance plays in representation. Further, documentaries refrained from singling any one film out as "the" black film. Hence, to gain a more nuanced understanding of Collins's films, it is important to locate them in the range of films available at that time. Forster's comments on the films makes a bold claim for them: "Understated in form, the series' selections present the revolutionary possibilities of ordinary black life in an anti-black world" (Forster 2015: 64). The "understated" form is a little enigmatic; the Collins films are almost excessively careful about form. The understatement perhaps refers to a sustained attention to the story as distinct from an emphasis on visual imagery and effects. The series also featured television shows that were compilations of news stories—for example, *Inside Bedford Stuyvesant (1968–71)*—thereby presenting the black subject's daily reality. As discussed through the following chapters, the placement of the black subject in film as antagonist to the white subject and white America has been destructive, and even where the films were resistant, black subjects themselves were unidimensional—defined with reference to white subjects. The "revolutionary" potential in these films then refers to the everyday difficulties and small transcendences that mark black subjects as both black and human, the visible attrition because of the constant friction in the most mundane of activities, and the momentary richness in the enjoyment of human connections. Collins's films fall into this broad category. The screening of *Losing Ground* in the series excited the most press attention, partly because twenty years after it has been made, audiences are willing to accept its parameters, not necessarily with reference to class—the *Cosby Show* had done that—but because of its feminist *and* intellectual dimensions. And notwithstanding the release of Julie Dash's *Daughters of the Dust* (1991) to widespread critical acclamation, Collins's film and its philosophical edge emerges as "original" and "new." The Lincoln Center screenings do Collins a service in securing her place among the New York Black Independents: firstly, because the films are no longer "buried," and secondly, because their originality can be appreciated without their being relegated as curiosities. Forster concludes his piece on the screenings:

> What makes *Tell It Like It Is* so insightful is not merely that it features *Losing Ground* but that it contextualizes its screening within a specific era when a community of black filmmakers working in New York established a sort of underground production studio. (Forster 2015: 69)

During the 80s the New York Black Independents were able to secure funding from some government sources, and television distribution was considered worth trying and securing, but for real support, the artists turned to each other.

Figure 1.1 *Ganja and Hess*: Inhabiting the landscape

Efforts to establish the New York Black Independents is ongoing. *Black Camera* of Spring 2018 posted a call for papers for a special issue on the New York Black Independents with Collins featuring prominently. The effort is in part restitutive, to credit black filmmakers on the east coast of the US, to understand their institutional positions, and to recognize their aesthetics as distinct from those of the Los Angeles Independents. *Black Camera*'s description is worth quoting in full for an understanding of the differences between the cinematic practices of the New York Black Independents, and the Los Angeles "rebels," and for the place Collins has in the New York group, fast being recognized as a "school":

> Figures like Gunn and Collins, who were once pejoratively characterized as "belonging to the Hudson River school of cinematography" turned to both the stage and page as writers, sculpting worlds of middle-class black life that cut across time and prescribed notions of legible blackness. (*Black Camera* 2018: 6)

The key word "legible" bears expansion. The suggestion is that the New York Black Independents do not represent blackness in highly readable ways, the inference here being that other filmmakers take recourse to recognizable signifiers of blackness that reify dominant notions implicitly, if not explicitly. Feminist filmmakers such as Gurinder Chadha were later to rely on a strategy of "layering" cultural imagery to bolster the context of subaltern subjects without making them stereotypically readable.

Landscape provides the context for the characters in *The Cruz Brothers*, presenting viewers with a familiar context in mainstream high culture but less so in the African American cultural context. The "Hudson River School of cinematography" carries derogatory values; the filmmakers were summarily dismissed for their ostensible romanticization of nature and their escape from reality to a pre-industrial Romantic past. The special issue seeks to redress this grievance. The interest in the landscape that Collins's *Cruz Brothers* and Bill Gunn's *Ganja and Hess* (1973) show flies in the face of a strictly representational, overtly politicized program for black filmmakers.

Even as there are elements of the Romance genre in Collins's two films and in *Ganja and Hess*, they are deeply philosophical and offer a world view cognizant of race. Their investment in the other arts, whether theatre or writing, carried over to film, and in that sense the films, particularly Collins's, are indebted to the larger African/African American literary tradition at least as much as they are to African American film history. The LA School is not to be viewed as a total oppositional point, however, for as the call mentions, the New York Black Independents are their "analog" (*Black Camera* 2018: 6).

The LA rebellion implicitly followed Fernando Solanas and Octavio Getino's call for a "Third Cinema" that forcefully established the "essential integrity of black and so-called Third World film cultures" (Willemen 1994: viii). Seeking to change reactionary forces, filmmakers used anti-illusionist techniques to foreground the educational mission. Aspects of its aesthetic are derived from the Latin American Espinosa's notion of "imperfect cinema," one that is hard hitting, and avoids high production values. Both Third Cinema and imperfect cinema were open to endless revision of aesthetic strategies, and multiplication in other parts of the world, as long as the films were an "expression of a new culture and of social changes" (Willemen 1994: 8). Haile Gerima's *Bush Mama* (1974) is an example of the core values of the LA School, revealing as it does the grinding oppression of poverty, compounded with race, and gender that the protagonist undergoes. Coming to UCLA after the Watts riots of 1965, Gerima also brought a consciousness of anti-colonial struggles that inflected the thinking of the group that studied writers such as Kenya's Ngugi and Martinique's Fanon (Masilela 1993). Gerima's film is grainy and has the quality of newsreel footage, arresting in producing the look of a "New Wave" of African American film. Charles Burnett's film *Killer of Sheep* (1977) is quite different in quality, and has neither the pace nor the almost panicked feeling of *Bush Mama*. The film opens with footage that is reminiscent of the Italian neo-realists, long tracking shots establishing the city, the train tracks and the children playing in odd, beaten-down neighborhoods. The film is almost authentically realist in the Lukácsian sense of the term, describing social conditions completely, and the alienation of the working-class protagonist from his working conditions. It shows working-class consciousness but not the working class rising. Instead, despite the resistance to the conditions expressed in symbols, there is almost a sense of despair, the montage of the heads of sheep intruding on the protagonist's interiority. The use of blues music as an aesthetic further marks the difference of this film from others that used realism. *Bush Mama* and *Killer of Sheep* together offered models of realism in African American film that were a departure from previous films, and that were to remain largely anomalous even as the mainstream New Realism city films were released.

Several differences can be discerned when comparing these two films with Bill Gunn's *Ganja and Hess* and Collins's two films. Firstly, while some of the New York filmmakers knew each other, they were not part of a collective in the way the LA Independents were. For instance, under the aegis of the film scholar Teshome Gabriel, the UCLA students studied with Glauber Rocha, who had theorized the Cinema of Hunger (Masilela 1993). Secondly, both New York filmmakers turned to a range of genres and devices to impart philosophical ideas. Thirdly, they were invested in writing, and as is apparent in their films, bringing writing to film. Fourthly, neither of them appears committed only to cityscapes but feature landscapes outside the city. Finally, their protagonists seek a rich personal understanding of their place in the world. Both film directors lend a lot of credence to art, literature, and philosophy as topics for films, and deploy them as discursive tools in the film to get their ideas across, or to flesh out their ideas in narrative. None of the three films insists on the purely realistic, but they use realism, more so in the case of *Losing Ground* than in the other two.

Bill Gunn of *Ganja and Hess* played the role of the artist husband of Sara in *Losing Ground*, Duane Williams of *The Night of the Living Dead* played Duke, and Seret Scott, a stage actor for whom Collins had written plays, was cast as Sara Rogers, the philosophy professor. At first glance, *Ganja and Hess* could not be further from Collins's films. A vampire/horror/parody of Blaxploitation film, it is free of all vestiges of cinematic realism. Yet, if one were to apply Collins's own idea that the difficulty for the filmmaker was to find "narrative solutions" to tell the story or convey philosophical ideas, Gunn had hit upon an unusual cinematic cocktail to offer a grounded view of race on the United States (Collins [1980] 2015).

Ganja and Hess is allegorical and has a Christian overlay, reminiscent of Spencer Williams's *The Blood of Jesus* (1941). Yet, Christianity is not the only component of the African American protagonist's identity; he is also influenced by his African past, visually depicted in the various African artefacts that contrast the european art work in the settings of the film. Dr. Hess Green's "blood" connection to Africa is also explored: he has been infected by a dagger of the ancient black Myrthian people. He was stabbed by a stranger with the dagger three times, "Once for the Father, once for the Son, and once for the Holy Ghost." Hess is a student of this ancient African tribe that is extinguished because of a blood disease. Plot expedients aside, the premise of the film reveals the horror of race in the US: blacks are bled for their work, and never allowed to die. Slaking the rage that this inspires with blood is an incomplete solution but one that very temporarily offers the rest that endless work denies. The film's setting offers a Romance palette: long and wide shots of beautiful natural settings, an equally grand house replete with African works of art, owned by an anthropologist and archivist, served by a butler. The butler's subservience is closer to obeisance; yet, the role is played straight. Diawara and Klotman believe that Hess's wealth shows him up for the materialist he is, and further that the film critiques this materialism; rather, the set-up appears to be an imagining of an atavistic regal African past with Hess playing that role (Diawara and Klotman 1990). James E. Hinton's cinematography is lush and at times threatens to abandon the story.

The shots are lengthy and, because each sequence is introduced slowly, add to the density of the allegorical. One critic argues that Hinton's hapticity draws the viewer in to appreciate the texture of film itself; however, the blood spatters and the different hues of red after each vampire episode could equally distance the viewer, and alienate him or her in the Brechtian sense, and compel him or her to shift from the visual to a deeper consideration of the allegory (Jackson 2018). While Ganja, the female, is a dominant character, she is not exactly folded into the philosophical frame that seems to legitimize both Hess's vampirism and his lack of ethics. A long interlude focuses on Hess's assistant, played by Bill Gunn, reading and writing before he commits suicide, adding to the film's philosophical and inter-arts perspective an important aspect of the aesthetic of the New York Black Independents.

When *Ganja and Hess* is placed side by side with *Losing Ground*, the versatility of the New York Black Independents is made apparent. Collins does venture into the territory of spirit possession, a theme culled from Africa and its diaspora, but her film has a realistic overlay that falls short of the allegorical. As Gunn's protagonist is an institutional academic, so is her protagonist, a professor of philosophy. Reading and writing, its centrality to human thinking, is overtly foregrounded in *Losing Ground*, texts and philosophers explicitly referenced: Africa is symbolized by the book in both films, *Afrique Noir* in *Ganja and Hess* and Louis Mars's *The Crisis of Possession in Voodoo* in *Losing Ground*. In both films, art and philosophy are intertwined, with art being preponderant in *Ganja and Hess*, philosophy underlying the film, while art and philosophy enjoy equal prominence in *Losing Ground*, philosophy theorizing art. Both Collins and Gunn use nature as a trope in their films—Gunn in *Ganja and Hess* and Collins in both of hers—distinguishing them from many of the other New York Black Independents.

Collins is, however, very different from the male New York Black Independents in her deep awareness of the exclusion of black women as full human beings in film. She was sensitive to what she regarded as the "potent male imagery" in the trope of "adventure" films in the mainstream industry, including the slough of Blaxploitation films such as *Shaft*[2] (dir. Parks, 1971). She commends the turn to the interior journey in some black independent films but finds it disappointing that even the films that she thinks are radical in their expression of the complex humanity of black people posit "a kind of stagnant female impotence that is made poignantly clear" (Collins 1984b: 6). Singling out Burnett's *Killer of Sheep* and Lane's *A Place in Time* (1977) as films that delicately evoke "true pathos," and avoid the ignominious Stepin Fetchit archetype, she nevertheless finds that the female characters are "symbolic" (Collins 1984b: 6), and concludes that even these two rare films view women as stepping stones in the male adventure: "Yet how sad that in the end, we are still left with stagnant female souls hovering aimlessly around the male universe. How limiting is the idea that only men despair; Women [sic] can only comfort" (Collins 1984b: 17). Spike Lee's Nola Darling in *She's Gotta Have It* could definitely be regarded as a female adventurer; yet, not one who voyages into the interior landscape when compared with Burnett's and Lane's male heroes.

Among the New York Black Independents, Spike Lee is probably the best known not merely for his enormous output since *She's Gotta Have It* but also for having expressed his affiliation with New York in his films. One of the chief mise-en-scènes of the film, the protagonist's apartment carries the inter-arts theme discussed earlier. A large, aesthetic space, with Nola's collages or her newspaper cuttings pasted on the walls, the apartment is metonymic of Nola's attractiveness. Nola works as a paste-up artist and is an independent woman. As in *Ganja and Hess*, *She's Gotta Have It* begins with the written word, a literary epigraph from Zora Neale Hurston, one that frames the female in sympathetic terms but also one that distinguishes quite clearly between male and female desire. Lee's film is about a black female and her life, inviting comparison with Collins's *Losing Ground*. Shot in black and white film, *She's Gotta Have It* is innovative in using a narrative scheme to assemble a group portrait of a woman, Nola Darling, who lives on her own and has multiple male sexual partners. Lee uses direct cinema techniques to characterize Nola as fresh, engaging, and a woman living on her own terms; she is not anyone's "girl." The film is wry and mocks the men slyly, deflecting their narrative authority, as they are among the primary narrators of Nola Darling's story. The tension in the film is between Nola's refusal to cede sole proprietorship of her body to one of her three sexual partners, and their insistence that she should. The assumptions of the film, the philosophy that Nola starts and ends by espousing, are enjoying new life as a Netflix show. However, the philosophy is subsumed by the dominance of the male presence in the film. The men themselves reductively believe Nola is just greedy—her punishment, rape. The film slips out of the philosophical mode with the attack on Nola. Further, over the course of the film, Nola's autonomy that secured her sexuality is now reversed when her autonomy is challenged by her sexuality.

National Public Radio's reviewer offers a comparison on how the two films have withstood the passage of time: "Lee's and Collins's films are both about female liberation, but it's *Losing Ground* that's truly grounded in the struggle of achieving it, a crucial element that makes it no less revelatory now, 30 years after it was made" (Hachard 2015). That the film is still considered a revelation is a sign of how unthinkable Collins's treatment of the themes was in the 1980s and its consequent relative obscurity, while Lee's, perhaps more obviously fitting the notion of "female liberation," was widely hailed. Notwithstanding Lee's innovative film techniques, and the ideas Nola in *She's Gotta Have It* forwards, feminist critics of the time have uniformly been extremely critical of Lee's representation of the female figure. Jacquie Jones, for instance, considers Nola, played by Tracy Camilla Johns, a "fantasy." Comparing this role with one she plays in Mario Van Peebles's *New Jack City* (1991) as a mob boss's girlfriend, Wallace notes that "Johns's roles best represent the ambiguity between and the narrowness of the two categories that Black women are allowed to occupy in this cinema—that of the bitch and that of the 'ho" (Jones 1992: 96).

Although *New Jack City* is a mainstream film, *She's Gotta Have It* was not, underscoring the dearth of complex black female characterization, whether in independent film or mainstream. Collins herself wrote a "manifesto" about the lack of female figures in the films made by black independents at large (Williams 1994; Collins 1984b). Perhaps this is why Nola Darling is dubbed "the mother of the black female character" in the 1990s (Jones 1992); further, as recently as 2017 a blogger says that "[she admires] Nola Darling's characteristics of being a woke black woman" (Colclough 2017). Granted, some of the ideas Nola expresses are "woke," and the director tries to demystify the male gaze through postmodern techniques, but the male narrative in the text excludes female narrative. Collins's *Losing Ground* made five years earlier deals with female desire in a register that questioned its conflation with sexual desire, but links it to many other pleasures, some sensory, some intellectual, but clearly connected to something extraordinary outside of carnal sex: "ecstasy" in one or all its variants. The sequences in *Losing Ground* that are most associated with experiencing rapt pleasure are not unmixed with other sensations, of doubt, of anguish. The trope of female pleasure, embedded in the erotic, is not a topic explored by mainstream films, invested as they are in the pursuit of male pleasure and adventure. Although there are instances of female pleasure and satisfaction in some feminist films, such as *Hour of the Star* by Suzana Amaral (1985), these are usually only fleeting within the diegesis of the film. Collins's film is perhaps more expansive in including more than one sequence showing female pleasure in a concerted unified way, a pleasure that has rarely been given voice even in women's literature. A notable exception is Marguerite Duras in both *Le ravissement de Lol V. Stein* (1964) and *L'Amant* (1984). The Jean-Jacques Annaud film of the same name (1992) is hard put to translate that female desire and pleasure to film, the very visual qualities of the novel being hyper-exaggerated by the film to no good effect. Curiously, although the theme of female pleasure was not touched upon, one of the very few commentaries on Collins refers to Duras and the genre and techniques of the

New Novel as analogous to Collins's approach in *Losing Ground* (Williams 1994). Among feminist philosophers, Luce Irigaray's and Monique Wittig's writings on female desire and pleasure resonate with Collins's approach, particularly the notion that the language to express such female desire and passion has yet to be found (Irigaray 1985b; Wittig 1976).

Lee's 1989 *Do the Right Thing*, like *She's Gotta Have It*, also, to some extent, casts the city itself as a character, almost anthropomorphizing it. The opening sequence of *She's Gotta Have It* is a series of sepia-tinted shots of people, particularly children, on the streets of New York. Lee's more extensive use of the city in *Do the Right Thing* places him in that group of great urban filmmakers: Lang for Berlin, Rossellini for Rome, Truffaut for Paris, among others. His love affair with the city, specifically what he calls "The Republic of Brooklyn," emerges in almost all of his films (Sterritt 2007). Collins's *Losing Ground* is set partly in New York City, but the city is only a background, not a central element as it is in Lee's films, exhibiting the different strands followed by the Independents.

Where *She's Gotta Have It* shows a Nola occupying spaces in the city with the freedom of an independent woman, *Do the Right Thing* focuses on Mookie, played by Lee, walking up and down the streets of Brooklyn delivering pizzas. A comparison of *Do the Right Thing* with *The Cruz Brothers and Miss Malloy* indicates very different philosophies of race, and equally different approaches to filmmaking. *Do the Right Thing* features a "sympathetic racist," Sal, the owner of the pizzeria whose impatience with a young black man's blaring radio incites a violent confrontation that ends with the young man, Radio Raheem, being killed by the police (Flory 2006). The conclusion is open to interpretation: Mookie throws a trash can into the pizzeria's window, either in hoping to appease the crowd's thirst for revenge, or in a feeble effort to show that he stands with the community although he works for the pizzeria. The film is intricate in showing communities in New York other than the African American: the Puerto Ricans are a part of the group, if not completely integrated; a vignette of the

Korean American store accentuates the different positionalities of minorities in the community. Lee shows the fault-lines in the community, particularly the sense of the black community becoming "woke" over issues of representation. The black clients of the pizzeria are beginning to question the complete absence of African Americans in Sal's photographic displays of Italian Americans. The film is organized around some binaries—love/hate, MLK Jr/Malcolm—but the cleverness of the film is in not getting into the binary of black/white, and rather showing the institutional power of white authority aligning itself with the light-skinned migrant, the Italian. Realistic, the film is rooted very much in the local, and although not dated, it is very much of its time. Any statement on race is made through the action of the film itself, organized around the unities of time, place, and action, and complete with a Brooklyn Mayors Chorus of old men commenting on the action, overseen by a Sister Mother from a second floor embrasure, a being from on high.

Both *The Cruz Brothers* and *Losing Ground* depict a multi-ethnic community in and around New York City, and in Rockland and Westchester Counties. Collins routes race through the personal stories of her characters, not the other way around. The city itself seems less inhabitable than Lee's Brooklyn with its houses, its steps, and its streets that the residents claim as their "own," however erroneously. A Puerto Rican in New York City, Celia, in *Losing Ground*, leaves the city after two years to come to Rockland County. She claims that she hates New York and that it smells. In *The Cruz Brothers*, the three young Puerto Rican men move to a place outside the city, their refrain: "At least it's not the Bronx." The Bronx is something they have left behind, and while they do not elaborate on the difficulties of the urban, they remember those experiences. In their new place, José says, "That's still amazing, living in this sweet little town, not the Bronx . . ." Collins emphasizes their joy in the house that brings them a feeling of inclusion, their pleasure in basic living conditions not possible for them in the city. In some senses, this new place outside the city affords them a chance at life; unlike the city that, we are to believe, both separated the brothers and swallowed them. Details of the debris in their house are contrasted with the setting. From their living quarters, the brothers can see pale greenery, some of it artfully landscaped, with a view towards the distant hills. The many shots of the landscape are effected with an eye to creating an artistic palette, nature itself symbolically representing the unspoken aspirations of the brothers. As an element in the film, nature functions ideologically and, in the best traditions of the Romance genre, is beneficent. At the narrative level, the satisfaction of the brothers with this new town outside the city throws a glare on the absent narrative of the city, suggesting an abyss in contrast to the plenitude of nature. That unspoken abyss is race. Collins's philosophical premise that the ordinary life story needs to be narrated without constant reference to race, although race is ever-present, sometimes determining, sometimes flexible, results in films that insist on connections between the internal—self—and the external—race (Collins 1984a).

New York figures prominently again in Charles Lane's *A Place in Time* and his later *Sidewalk Stories* (1989). Both titles signal the centrality of place to the films. The opening epigraph of *A Place in Time* accepts the inevitability of the city as an agonist, evoking the "empty streets," the "loneliness," the "coldness" as a "part of our place in time." In a street corner on a sidewalk by Astor Place in Broadway, an artist and a dancer try to eke a living. Both films are shot in an extremely realistic style in black and white and recall the crispness of Walter Ruttmann's city images in *Berlin: Symphony of a Great City* (1927). The anonymity of the city, its indifference to its inhabitants, is a chilling factor in the films that reveal the human cost of this ethos; however, in paying homage to the silent cinema, particularly Charlie Chaplin, the films also produce "humanistic" comedy (Mast and Kawin 2011). Their philosophy folds race into the other qualities that make the protagonist an artist and an outsider: his poverty, his homelessness, his kindness, his humor. *Sidewalk Stories* follows a street artist as he tries to survive in the city. Witnessing a murder, the artist takes the victim's young child to safety and lives in various abandoned sites, becoming more and more involved with taking care of the child. That human contact in the isolation of the city suffuses the film with joy, and even when race rears its ugly head, as it does when the artist takes the child to public facilities, he takes it in his stride. Ultimately, it is the loss of companionship that beats him down. Lane's philosophical premises are closer to Collins than they are to Lee. Of the risk *A Place in Time* took with its inept, tramp protagonist, Collins said, "It took my breath away" (Collins 1984b: 17). Both *The Cruz Brothers* and the Lane films celebrate the kind of alliances that can be forged across groups, whether of class or race. The male, single, homeless artist taking care of a child in *Sidewalk Stories* appears little short of completely unexpected as is the friendship in *The Cruz Brothers* between the wealthy, european american, octogenarian woman and the three hapless, Puerto Rican young men.

The history of the New York Black Independents makes it clear that filmmaking was not an isolated activity; indeed, what distinguished the New York Black Independents was the range of inter-arts alliances in projects including drama, literature, painting, and photography. They were also proficient in the use of diverse formats such as video camera and alternate distribution channels, WNET New York Public Television being a primary outlet. Several of their films had been made on shoestring budgets and had received some federal funding. "Translations" from literature to film were also important, especially if the literary piece had resonated with audiences and touched on relevant topics. One such example of using dramatic or literary material is of Steve Carter's play, "One Last Look," a resource for Charles Hobson's film of the same name made in 1969. The play and film, when set side by side with Collins's plays and films, show the commonalities across the New York Black Independents.

One Last Look is about a family returning home for the funeral of their father to get some answers, to express their disappointment, and to take stock of their lives. The father appears as a ghost and engages in continuous dialogue with them. Collins also uses the funereal gathering as a setting for her play, "The Brothers," about a family coming together for the funeral of a family member, a world-famous athlete; the atmosphere and the conversation are quite similar to Carter's play, speaking to the commonality of the theme. Both address the difficulties of identity in the context of family history and ethnic community.

The appeal of presenting Carter's material from "One Last Look" on film involves a move away from realism, and the director, Hobson, chances it. Similarly, Collins, almost ten years later, settles on a non-realistic tale but goes further away for her source material—to a Jewish American writer, Henry Roth, for her film on three Puerto Rican young men and their ghost father for *The Cruz Brothers and Miss Malloy*. As in the Carter play and the Hobson film, "Poppa" interrupts continuously and refuses to die. The search for modes other than the realistic, then, was vital to these filmmakers in their desire to narrate the complexity of the lives of black subjects.

The connections between artists is patent in the "meta-soap opera" *Personal Problems* (1980–1) directed by Bill Gunn but with freewheeling license for all to collaborate. This openness to suggestions and lack of emphasis on the sole authority of the director was shared by Collins, who encouraged the participation of her cast and crew in the filming process. Ishmael Reed, the African American writer, was one of the producers, and in his notes on the Kino-Lorber release, he mentions that he traveled to DC to show it to staff members of PBS. Apparently, one staff member "disparaged" Bill Gunn and Kathleen Collins. Clearly, some of the New York Black Independents were associated with similar philosophies and aesthetics. The premise of Reed's project was open-ended in that the producers wished to respond to the black community's sense of itself, something that they were hungry to see. Reed's questions were: "What happens when a group of unbankable individuals tell their stories? Actors who have final say over their speaking parts? A director, who was found 'too difficult' for Hollywood?" The director that Reed is referring to is Bill Gunn (Reed [1980] 2018). Baldwin too had been expelled from Hollywood so there was some sense of urgency about countering Hollywood. Robert Polidori used ¾" U-matic tapes, and allowed the film to run after the scene was shot, using improvisation as a key aesthetic feature. The production history of *Personal Problems* is also illustrative of the links across media and artists among the New York Black Independents. Originally a radio soap opera, it had been funded by various local arts organizations and was recorded in producer Steve Cannon's apartment (Reed [1980] 2018).

The key features of the New York Black Independents can be summed up by (a) the diversity of formats and genres, (b) the richness of collaborations across artists of different media, and (c) the depth of support among filmmakers and artists. Kathleen Collins's films illustrate the kind of arrangements Independents had to make. Stage actor Seret Scott played the female lead role in *Losing Ground*, Bill Gunn and Duane Jones, professional actors, played the two male roles. Other organizational elements were equally makeshift, and each production a war waged against huge budgetary constraints. Collins had considerable experience in commercial editing, and had also worked on Larry Neal's 1969 *May Be the Last Time* (O'Malley 2019). Indeed, Kathleen Collins exemplified the mixture of talent that comprised the New York Black Independents who were actors, directors, editors, musicians, camera-persons, sometimes all at the same time. An academic, a writer of short fiction, a playwright with many plays behind her, author of film criticism, skilled film editor, Collins emerges as one of the central figures of the New York Black Independents.

Notes

1 Translation mine.
2 The series continues: a 2000 remake (dir. Singleton) and a 2019 film with the same title (dir. Story).

2

The black essai film

In the context of the US in the 1970s and 80s, the cinema-going public was, in general, not offered films that questioned the viewer's monochromatic beliefs about the lives of black people. As a culture, while mainstream and black audiences engaged with illusionistic adventure films, black independent filmmakers were making films that in any other national cinema circles would be called New Wave. Films produced by the LA movement and the New York Black Independents belong to this group of filmmakers, who devised a new aesthetics to "see some aspects of black reality accurately portrayed on the screen" to counter Hollywood's "blindness" (Mims 1990: 3). A cinema of ideas inevitably calls for a shift in the language of mainstream film, whether it is at the level of the elements of filmmaking, the narrative trajectory, or the aesthetic modes that are used. Collins strives to achieve the precision of the written word in her narrative design, bending the language of cinema to philosophical use. A reviewer suggests that this aesthetic is reminiscent of the French New Wave's ideological orientation. Commenting on *Losing Ground*, the reviewer identifies a subtle but direct dialectic around an "intellectual university professor" as the film's "primary quality," or its écriture (SD; translation mine). Yet, Collins's films, while similar in their efforts to make the language "new" and in their overall literary impetus, are based on premises that are substantially different from the corpus of a Rohmer or a Varda.

The majority of French New Wave films assume both the security of a post-World War II economy and the settledness of the western philosophical framework. Agnès Varda differs slightly in that she follows people marginal to mainstream bourgeois culture, vagabonds, migrants, artists. While Collins also reveals an abiding interest in outsiders, particularly women as outsiders, unlike Varda, she does not focus exclusively on eliciting knowledge about the individual but thinks through what it means to belong to a community of outsiders. Both are preoccupied with narrative structure as crucial to altering the stories we tell of women. Varda concentrates on multiple narrative perspectives that attempt to understand the gap between interiority and exteriority, as in *Vagabond* (1985). In her two films, *The Cruz Brothers and Miss Malloy* (1980) and *Losing Ground* (1982), Collins retains the authenticity of the interior vision of her characters without allowing narrative to overcome the philosophical thread of the film.

Comparing Collins's aesthetic to the French director she most admired, Éric Rohmer, also suggests some key differences. Take *My Night with Maud* (1969), one of the six moral tales Collins mentions as having had the greatest influence on her (Nicholson 1988/9). The running argument in the film and the "conte," or story, is over Pascal and his beliefs. The dialogue circles around the question of a moral choice. The male character, who appears to believe that his destiny is elected and therefore that his choices can only be moral, does not understand that subtlety in moral choice also lies in how one responds to the choice someone else has made. These discussions are held very much within the context of beliefs in the elegant, ultimately mathematical world questioned by women but controlled by men. The filming is similarly polished and quiet in having no protuberances; the form following the belief that moral order, even when troubled, exists. The characters themselves may experience radiant, mystical fullness of being through their encounter with each other; however, their knowledge emerges from the depth of their belonging to that western philosophical tradition and their well-defined awareness of its contribution to humanity. Race, or even difference as such, is a non-factor, driving home the notion that humanness is defined by their knowledge of self and a sense of accord with someone akin to them as in the case with the protagonists of the film. Thus, the film is overtly philosophical in essaying an argument.

An influential philosophical departure point for Collins is Jean-Paul Sartre's *Saint Genet: Actor and Martyr* ([1952] 1963). She understands his notion of the Christian "transformation of the sinner into the saint" to underlie the social imperative to construct sinners/outsiders; in the US context, African Americans, gays, lesbians, and other people forced to occupy the metaphysical place of the sinner, the social space of the outsider. The philosophical urgency for Collins, then, is to find forms of "transformation" that do not divide the world into sinners and saints. To explore these possibilities, she brings an entirely new set of philosophical references, and incorporates race within a world literature frame that includes, among others, Louis Mars, Jean Genet, African American folklore, and Puerto Rican popular culture (Collins 1984a).

The abstractness of Collins's films results in plots that are both pinned to and unpinned from external and internal motivations alike. The title *Losing Ground* intimates that there will be no neat resolution, the plot ungrounded. The female hero, a philosophy professor, gives a lecture; she goes with her artist husband to upstate New York and acts in a film that a student, George, makes. The pinning to the exterior is loosened by the absorption in the intensity of the protagonist's interior life translated by the theatrical mise-en-scènes.

The format that Collins uses invites us to see black characters outside of the blackface camouflage, and Latinx characters within the national imaginary. It is not that the "look is returned" as in many subaltern films. The Hegelian dialectic, a violence Irigaray finds innate to vision, is not apparent in Collins's use of visuality as a trope in the diegesis (Irigaray 1985a). Equally importantly, she does not rely on the relay of looks to build her narrative. The bracketing of vision in feminist film reveals the hostility of the medium to women as in Nelly Kaplan's *The Pirate's Fiancée* (1969) where the protagonist outrages the voyeur. Collins, however, amplifies the possibilities of vision, augmenting the physicality of vision with the metaphysical. She achieves this meta-commentary on vision without taking recourse solely to the trajectory of looks but by lingering on the objects—painting and the printed word—that the characters look at. Consequently, the philosophical location of vision is detached from received imagery on African Americans. Thus, Collins appears to overwrite film as the negative scene of instruction for African Americans.

Music, the positive scene of instruction in African American culture, and auditory mechanisms amplify the thematic of existential exploration in relation to exterior conscriptions of what identity ought to entail, race, gender, and class affiliation (Wallace 1993b: 212). Identity in *Cruz Brothers* is explored through interactions with the other and with the ancestor. Victor, the oldest son in *Cruz Brothers*, listens to his father who talks only to him, giving him advice on how to survive in a world of white people whom one cannot trust.[1]

Through the course of the films, the interior landscape is shown to be more important as the films substitute the dilemma for the enigma, or the desire of the plot. Certainly, many Third Cinema films are explicitly and self-consciously organized around the dilemma, whether of race or class, as in the Brazilian Cinema Novo and Glauber Rocha's Cinema of Hunger, among others. While this holds for Collins's films, the inflection, here, is on the dilemma of how to reconcile the interior landscape with the external ground. Sara's research on the possibility of experiencing otherworldly ecstasy is obscure for a black woman living in the US in the 1980s. Victor of *The Cruz Brothers* is presented as a hustler turned ethnographer. Both films do not offer resolutions, but the characters do have a mystical experience that affords them a greater understanding even when the difficulties of everyday life persist.

Collins's approach to that intangible but all important task of rendering black and Latinx characters out of the various straitjackets into which they have been placed in US film is achieved in a different mode than the two great paradigms of African American filmmaking that Manthia Diawara identifies, the expressive and the realist: the expressive organized around spatial narration, the realist temporal (Diawara 1993: 3–25). Collins uses elements from both paradigms, but the impact that both her films make owes much to her incorporation of the other arts of theatre, painting, and music. Collins's framework is philosophical in that her departure point is the questioning of the human subject, not the black human subject. Separating the two would seem to be grievous; an impossible fission that she explores in all its facets of otherness from the self. The artist/intellectual is unabashedly at the center of her films: the struggle of becoming a humanist artist and of getting to the bone of it without being marred by racial and gender barriers.

The history of African Americans in mainstream US film highlights the significance of Collins's ability to show black intellectuals and human subjects in environments other than the purposefully degrading. Both films have mise-en-scènes that fly in the face of other locations blacks are seen in, thus normalizing their right to inhabit artistic, intellectual aesthetic spaces. Seeing these characters in spaces that are luminous, such as the apartment Sara and Victor rent in upstate New York, deflects the Cartesian and the european american viewer's expectations of irreducible difference. The dialogue of *Losing Ground* interpolates the viewer when Victor mocks himself by saying that he is now a bonafide "Negro success" because he has won an award. The lead character of the film, Sara, again oversets expectations by not discussing her role as a black female intellectual but by talking about existentialism to her students, and about the relationship between female desire and the intellect with her mother, herself an actor. Sara's desire to desire, a trope in feminist films, is startling because black women are invariably presented as entertainers, highly sexualized, and seductive when not playing the defeminized mammy role.

Collins's sense of over-arching universalism that allows her to use extreme performance elements without compromising the humanity of her characters exists in part because of a primary acknowledgment of others as human before bracketing them into categories of race, gender, or class and other elements that define identity in much sharper lines. It is instructive to draw out the differences between universalism and cosmopolitanism. Post-structuralist discourse discredited the construction of the universal human subject in Enlightenment philosophy by enumerating the subjects the universal excluded: women, third world subjects, indigenous and black peoples. Consequently, the use of the term universal was jettisoned in academic writing, subaltern discourse preferring to locate identities within specific historical formations. While this was a much needed corrective, it excluded subaltern people from the category of the universal, handing it over to the west european white male. The multiplicity and specificity of the many differences among people became de rigueur, dividing subaltern groups from drawing useful comparisons and claiming universal subjecthood for themselves. Kathleen Collins bridges these differences without sacrificing cultural or historical specificity to restore the value of the universal in thinking of marginal subjects and their communities. Universalism continues to be generally dismissed for its political naïveté, with academics of different stripes deploying cosmopolitanism as a category within which to understand identity formation in the context of racial and cultural difference.

Over the last ten years "cosmopolitanism" has been quietly introduced as a new movement (Walkowitz 2006; Cheah and Robbins 1998). It could be argued that borrowings from many cultures, including the migrant and diaspora populations, comprise the cosmopolitanism of the metropolitan inhabitant, while metropolitan settings and the ease with which the stranger/migrant/non-native traverses these constitute the non-native's cosmopolitanism. This characterization is contested by "ethical" narratives of cosmopolitanism that address the notion of exchange between diverse cultures.

Feminist understandings of cosmopolitanism and feminism have, in general, diverged from other received discourses on the same. Cosmopolitanism appears very often to be allied with other movements that lean towards the masculine, if not being dominated by it. Western definitions of cosmopolitanism, largely linked to modernity and modernism, place the male flâneur at the center of this urban experience, with women signifying the cosmopolitanism of the urban but having restricted access to it. And despite the seemingly overarching sweep of the term, it means different things across different places. Very often the term is used as one of opposition to nationalism, as Gilroy defines it with reference to W. E. B. Du Bois, but as he himself concedes, Du Bois's African sensibility and his rootedness in African American culture make the definition rather shapeless (Shelby and Gilroy 2008). In her novels, the South African writer Bessie Head very often aligns it with male modernity, as in *Maru* (1971) where the tribal chief wants to make radical changes in women's conditions but without their consent and in his own interests. Unlike western critics of nationalism, Head does not believe that cosmopolitanism is less nationalistic; rather, it is more nationalistic by virtue of its post-colonial male foundation that excludes women and migrants, as in *When the Rain Clouds Gather* (1987). Whose cosmopolitanism? Male cosmopolitanism, whether it is in the global north or the global south. Universalism— across cultures, castes, races—is of greater value. Collins articulates this sentiment in her critique of Lorraine Hansberry. Pointing to Hansberry as a deep and lasting influence on her thinking and her work, Collins critiques Hansberry's commentary for pigeon-holing her despite the richness and range of her writings. She expresses "shock" at Hansberry's reach and says:

> She had a really incredible sense of life that fascinates me. That anything in life was accessible for her to write about... Instead of feeling that the Black experience was the only experience that she could write about. And it is that breadth of vision that I have always sensed was ultimately my vision. (Nicholson 1988/9: 8)

Collins's statement here and her conclusion that no other writer has mattered so much to her is a hailing of Hansberry's universalist approach to writing, based on Hansberry's apprehension of life. For Collins, such scope, which she pinpointed as being derived from world literature, was her natural habitation as artist. The choice then was less between what is now termed post-racial art and racial art than between cosmopolitanism and universalism. Universalism prompted her choice of characters, key to her representational practices that absorbed realism, modernism, and magical realism. That Collins was not wedded to received understanding of "realistic" representations of black and minority subjects does not imply a movement away from black politics. She regarded the question of whether film should be political or artistic as largely extraneous, stating that her films were political with a small "p," recognizing the political dimensions of the ethical and the aesthetic, in form as much as in content (Franklin 1981: 33).

The reach for the universal in lieu of the cosmopolitan is seen in the themes of *The Cruz Brothers*. Written by a Jewish American author, the story is about three Puerto Rican youths who are anything but cosmopolitan, and their interaction with an Irish American lady living in a grand house belonging to a bygone era. Collins tracks slowly through the sleepy upstate New York town in its determined, close-eyed whiteness and purposefully juxtaposes this by placing the wealthy New York socialite with the three barely working-class, hoop-playing boys in the crumbling interior of her mansion. She contrasts this mise-en-scène with the place the boys occupy, and yet the effect is not Eisensteinian; rather, it is to trace a universal line between characters whose social circumstances are dramatically different. The sequences in the house are shot with an aura of wonder, and do not exude the slightest whiff of the tawdry. The use of magical realism in these sequences is very light, but it is sufficient to suggest a connection in the real that links the characters and validates all of them in different ways. Like *Cruz Brothers*, *Losing Ground* shows the appeal of the universal, but it also sharply critiques a pretentious cosmopolitanism when Sara, in an uncharacteristic rage, accuses Victor, her artist husband, of invoking and exploiting cosmopolitanism for his own libidinal interests.

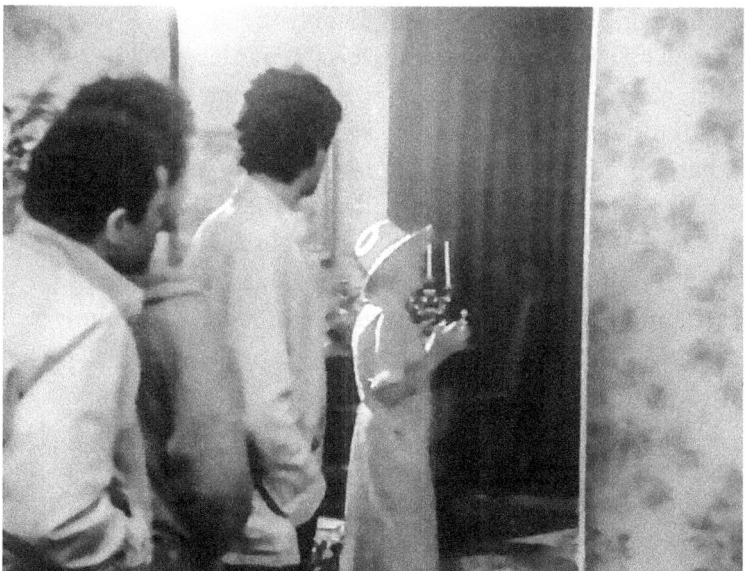

Figure 2.1 *Cruz Brothers*: The brothers in Miss Malloy's house

Collins's humanist framework that I call "universalism" distinguishes her from other cultural critics of the 1980s and 90s. For many, the category of universalism obviated the black experience, subsuming the black subject. Such indeed is the perspective of Du Cille's comments on the use value of black women's literature for european american feminist critics. According to her, the suffering and oppression of black women resonates with non-black women, who are encouraged and supported by the endurance of black women as revealed in black women's literature "to rise above not necessarily the pain of black women but of their own" (Du Cille 1994: 622). Du Cille has some objections to what could be regarded as an old trope in US literary history: the validation or authorization of black experience through the prism of white humanity:

> The griefs of African American women indeed seem to grieve on universal bones—"to concretize and make vivid a system of oppression." But it also seems (and herein lies the rub) that in order to grieve "universally," to be "concrete," to have "larger meaning," the flesh on these bones ultimately must always be white or male. (Du Cille 1994: 622)

Within this genealogy Collins is different in not insisting on specificity but demanding a universality for black subjects, their existence as overreaching narrow social and representational straits. The two points of view are not in contention with each other; I bring up Du Cille's argument merely to accent Collins's vision, which is unlike that of the binaries that doxa assumes. Where Du Cille believes that the specific is being nullified to contribute to a "false" universal—in actuality, a specific that is appropriated—Collins's struggle is to redeem the universal for the specific and to reinstate the universal in lieu of the cosmopolitan.

Collins's demand for an absolute universal for the black subject is not in and of itself a radical principle but becomes one when black subjects and their stories enter public discourse from assigned places to offer grist to the humanist mill. Black and third world feminist criticism was to point out the phenomenon by which all third world texts—and many, such as bell hooks, would argue that black texts in the US are third world texts—were treated as raw material to be turned into finished goods by the western theory mills (Ramanathan and Schlau 1995). In this, hooks's conclusion is no different than Du Cille's suspicion of the universal, but for Collins the filmmaker, dramatist, and writer of fiction, it was imperative to create that speaking space for her subjects that would be universal (hooks 1995)

The representational space afforded to black artists and painters by the critical community's persistent hailing of race was oblivious to differences across race, demanding an "authenticity" that tiresomely depended on US whiteness as the ultimate referent. Black artists of that time resisted that idea, recognizing that the limits placed on authentic blackness to (realistic) representation of black subjects would inhibit the invention/creation of a black tradition (Mercer 1994; hooks 1995). Collins acknowledges that historically black women are different from white women, but she is hesitant to decide on that basis alone on the definitiveness of a common black aesthetic:

> I would think that there is a Black aesthetic among Black women filmmakers. Black women are not white women by any means; we have different histories, different approaches to life, and different attitudes. Historically, we come out of different traditions; sociologically, our preoccupations are different. However, I have a lot of trouble with this question because I do not feel there has been a long enough tradition. (Reid 1993: 122)

The specificity of a black aesthetic, a black modernism, and black performativity are each separate and linked minefields. The black aesthetic has been linked variously to the Harlem Renaissance of the 1930s, the Black Arts Movement of the 1960s, and films such as *Looking for Langston* (dir. Julien, 1989). The earliest version of black modernism features black culture, oral arts, and literature in black expressive language, including the work of Zora Neale Hurston, Countee Cullen, Langston Hughes, and Jean Toomer, to name only a few. The 1960s movement was "radically opposed to any concept of the artist that alienated him from his community," and there was a strong belief that the aesthetics revealed the artist's ethics (Neal 1968: 28). Black performativity with reference to the post-60s movement used mimicry to hollow out received blackness and to find new forms of expressive blackness. The latter has a lot in common with postmodern interpretations of black visual culture. However, Collins offers a black aesthetic that is more amorphous; nevertheless, it has its roots in the Black Arts tradition that sought links to the third world, and the 1980s black modernist art that similarly had connections with the third world, and the African diaspora in particular. Her work is based on her own cultural experiences but also her aspirations for the universality of the black subject. The notion of black performance, while peculiarly a device and a trope in both her films, is to be distinguished from black performativity as parody; rather, black performance is elevating in the sense of bringing the actor to her/his existential self. Given the richness of drama during the Black Arts period, and Collins's work as a playwright, it stands to reason that she viewed performance as a mode to arrive at the everyday experiences of black and minority subjects. Collins's substantial dramatic oeuvre and her fiction is vital in showing her connections with a black women's literary movement in the 1980s and centers black women's communities and dialogues among black women, unfolding an almost exclusively black community.

Working within a world cinematic and literary tradition that is capacious lends Collins elements of her universalist philosophy. She is, for instance, an admirer of Gabriel García Márquez and has been emphatic about her singular devotion to Rohmer. The attention to language is the draw here. Collins contends that she is a "moralist," paying attention to the crucial but seemingly "slight moral issues" that one encounters in daily life (Kathleen Collins qtd in Okiti 2016: 38). In *Losing Ground*, Victor is confronted with the moral choice of discounting the concerns of a black female intellectual, who is also his wife, or giving her ideas serious consideration. "Emotional truth" and "purity" are important concepts for Collins, demanding as they do self-scrutiny and a certain authenticity in one's actions. The Cruz brothers are confronted with just such a moral choice when they meet a rich New Yorker who asks them to help refurbish her house. Are they to treat her as though she were nuts, or with dignity and respect without condescension? More importantly, they must feel this "emotional fact," or truth, not just play-act for decency's sake (Sara Rogers qtd in Okiti 2016: 38).

Collins's Weltanschauung was framed by her belief that the world was organized around the dichotomy of the saint and the sinner. Using Sartre's biography on Genet, she contends that social metaphysics requires sinners. Blacks have been defined as sinners, a trope that is extremely well realized in Genet's *The Blacks*, which covers passing, the Other, detachment from the body, and shock over the ludicrousness of color. In the metaphysical scheme Collins describes, it is important to project sinfulness onto an other, and to contrast the extra-ordinary evil of the sinner to the equally exaggerated holiness of the saint. Above all, Collins wishes to move people outside this framework and to arrive at a "normalcy," an "ordinariness" that she believes black people are denied. Neither film is constructed around the elevated drama of calamity, nor even the grandeur of tragedy where there is an extraordinary fall (Collins 1984a). There are moments of truth and redemption in both films: in the discoveries of Victor in *Cruz Brothers* and Sara in *Losing Ground* (Collins 1984a). Redemption is of course an element after the anagnorisis or recognition in tragedy. Here, the characters do not need to fall from a lofty height. Another way of philosophizing this "ordinariness" would be to suggest that Collins is looking to a "postcategorical utopia that is an impulse towards a world where the oppressive effects of identity categories" would not be the primary means of ascertaining one's humanity (Kilpeläinen 2012: 2).[2] However, Collins's ideas have little to do with the more conventional, loosely postmodern avoidance of grand narratives that the post-racial seems to signal. For Collins, race as a notional entity was very observable; the task was to unravel that notionality, and in her writing and films, she was able to write about characters who were aware of it, and to offer a range of responses, all of which she presents as humane and universal (Collins 2019).

Collins's rendition of what I am calling the "black essai" film exceeds the limits of the French essai film, and the black independents. One critic, in attempting to suggest differences between African American woman filmmakers of the 1980s and onwards, notes very pointedly that despite the fact that these women were college educated and the products of the civil rights moment, they did not feature black individuals pursuing college but journeyed into the past, into slavery. Among the filmmakers included in that study are Julie Dash, Euzhan Palcy, and Maureen Blackwood (Ryan 2005). To the contrary, Collins did show two individuals in *Losing Ground* who are very much part of an intellectual world. The motif of blackness as essence or essential heritage does not obtain with Collins as it may in these other films. Nevertheless, even as the "ancestral archive" seems of little specific importance to Sara in *Losing Ground*, she is very open to the "universal archive" and is invested in experiences that are not limited to the definable. In that aspect, the "double vision" unattributed to a specific black essence but very loosely attributed to a specific black epistemological project, not exclusively identity, cannot be gainsaid, whether it is *Losing Ground*'s Sara's attempts to explore her intellectual identity with respect to an abstract notional racial mountain, or Victor's conflicts with his absent/present father in *Cruz Brothers* about how Puerto Ricans in New York are expected to behave.

Critical reception of Collins's films has been attuned to their emphasis on interiority and hapticity, including their philosophical orientation, but problematic in not registering that the intellectual is central to her vision of the universal. However, the premise that the body untrammeled by race fosters the creation of a "metaphysical space" outside of the "intellectual," even if marked by "affect," boxes Collins into the very category of essence, even when this is designated as "post-black," not "post-racial" (Beverly 2012). Any overt rejection of the intellectual, or the idea that the intellectual does not include the "affect" or that the intellectual is solely rational misses the crux of the interior conflict in *Losing Ground*, where the female intellectual is denigrated for being intellectual and is challenged, by a male, to be essentially more "female." Thus, the philosophical challenge the film faced was to develop the idea of a *female* intellectual. The ostensible plot conflict in the film between the male and the female is played out on masculine ground. The male artist, without any nuance of hesitation or self-doubt, assumes that the artist's being and experience are ultimate, echoing the Aristotelian dictum about creativity and masculinity. Paradoxically, this point of view diminishes the intellectual when it is aligned with the female hero, for in her it is associated with rigidity and the lack of ability to be expressive. Sara feels self-doubt as a consequence of Victor's charges of inflexibility; however, it does not inhibit her from studying the "Ecstatic Experience." Collins's narrative scheme connects the intellectual to the expressive; the female hero's journey results in her linking the two. The male modernist artist in the diegesis appears decoupled from the intellectual even as the female intellectual incorporates the expressive.

The film follows the protagonist's search for ecstasy; "transport" and "rapture" are approximate synonyms. "Transport" is close to ecstasy except that the emotion it elicits is specified as "violent." "Rapture," while heavily contaminated today by the fundamentalist use of the term, has mystical inflexions, as defined by *Webster's New Collegiate Dictionary*: "Etymologically a seizing, in earlier use implied a lifting of the mind or soul by divine power, so that it might see things beyond the range of human vision." That Sara, as an intellectual, seeks to research the diverse experiences of ecstasy would appear to be anomalous, but it is in keeping with the desire of the narrative to expand the boundaries of the western intellectual quest. Very few feminist films or African American films, or indeed very few films at all, feature a female in search of ecstasy, inspiring one reviewer to express gratitude for this "recognition of intellectual ecstasy that is profoundly rare in the realm of ideas" (SD; translation mine).

Collins's route to the protagonist's ecstasy is through western and African philosophical thought, African American literature, and avant-garde film. She sets up philosophical propositions only to move away from them to other more complex statements that are universalist, rather than unitary, and specific. The film, in conjunction with the metafilm, proposes the inclusion of African gnosis to the western philosophy of the professor's classroom. The insistence on ways of knowing beyond the scopic, of knowing through the body, but not only through the body, serves as a feminist counterweight to western metaphysics.

The discussion on otherness started in the lecture hall continues in the library, gliding smoothly into the conversational exchange on ecstasy: a rare debate in the history of ideas, even rarer in film. The two mise-en-scènes that seem to demarcate the boundaries of knowledge—the lecture hall, and the library—are later shown to be insufficient as Sara absorbs crucial knowledge on ecstasy in the film set. In the library, Sara is reading with the utter absorption of one in a trance when she is interrupted by a stranger who wants to know what she is reading. When she tells the man, Duke, that she is writing a paper on "Ecstatic Experience," he wants to know whether it is from a theological standpoint. After their discussion on St. Theresa and the Gnostics' understanding of ecstasy, Sara advances her thesis that the "religious boundaries around ecstasy are too narrow." Duke, in turn, points out that the Christians are too restrictive regarding a human being's intuition. Duke also introduces the psychic dimension when he suggests that the Gnostics had that "orientation." The Gnostics' belief in knowledge as emancipatory is not entirely satisfying to Sara, who later visits a psychic, in essence to find out about herself. Both Duke and Sara reject the theological as the only dimension to provide an avenue to ecstasy; Sara's thesis includes the notion that "artists, for example, have frequent ecstatic experiences." Sara opts for a broader definition of the divine, one that involves a certain kind of possession, where the other is folded into the self, different from perhaps the grace offered by religious vision. Christian vision then is divisive, demanding a self and an other, a demarcated subject and object. Irigaray theorizes that vision, as distinct from hapticity, emphasizes the whatness of seeing, the object to be seen, in place of a mingling (Irigaray 1985a). The ideal of ecstasy modeled on vision is not suited to a philosophy professor who, despite her husband's slurs, is passionate and intuitive about a seemingly "rational" field, apologizing neither for her intellectualism, nor for her femininity and intuitiveness. Possession, in Christian terms, is usually a negative term. However, in African and eastern mystical traditions, it is a vital part of a mystical experience, whether religious or not.

Collins was well acquainted with the Haitian vaudun tradition, and had translated Louis Mars's book on the various stages of possession. Mars's treatise is detailed, not just in the practice but in the precise and careful stages in each of the levels of possession. The vaudun was equally part of the African American cultural tradition; for instance, Zora Neale Hurston, the anthropologist and writer, had traveled to Haiti, immersed herself in the practice of vaudun, and had written a book on it, *Tell My Horse: Voodoo and Life in Haiti and Jamaica* (1938). Collins would have known not only about Hurston's work but also of the avant-garde filmmaker Maya Deren's exalted experiences with vaudun in Haiti, published in 1953. Although these texts are not named in the film, Collins pulls from these archives to universalize philosophy by expanding the research on ecstasy. She synthesizes her ideas on the possibilities of ecstasy for a black intellectual woman by staging the dance/film/performance of her protagonist experiencing something close to being "beyond oneself."

The film within the film features the philosophy professor playing the role of a vaudeville performer, Frankie, and her lover and dance partner, Johnny. The motif itself is drawn from African American folklore. The final shot of the film is both diegetic and extra-diegetic, showing us Sara's husband, Victor, looking at Sara, even as we and Victor see Sara in the throes of a powerful concerted emotion, as Sara blows Johnny away. The audience intuitively understands that Victor too has been blown away. The act has an inevitability that rises to the tragic, and is in part a reprisal of an African American film, *Carmen Jones*, featuring Harry Belafonte and Dorothy Dandridge. In that film, Carmen pursues Joe, acquires every kind of emotional power over him, and then wishes to abandon him. Joe, in violent despair, strangles her. The film within the film reinscribes that melodrama, with the roles reversed but only in some aspects. While Joe is shot in terrifyingly bleak close-ups, and close-ups of Carmen reveal her plight, here, Sara, as Frankie, is composed, with Johnny not having a clue as to what is occurring. The films differ in that *Carmen Jones* follows in a long line of dramatic and literary male protagonists killing women. The violence in *Losing Ground* is enclosed in the extra-diegetic: Frankie shoots Johnny; Sara does not shoot Victor.

Where the revenge motif may be sufficient to demand for women the right to passion, even if violent, the extra-diegetic sequence accrues significance only because of the doubling

Figure 2.2 *Losing Ground*: Playing the role of Frankie

Figure 2.3 *Carmen Jones*: "I could have been another Dorothy Dandridge." Sara in *Losing Ground*

of Sara as Frankie. The use of the term "doubling" may be distracting. After all, do not all actors assume another role? Yes, they do, but not usually when they are already acting in a film. Parallels to the diegetic in the meta-dramatic or metafilmic

Figure 2.4 *Carmen Jones*: Violence against women

usually have the function of alerting both characters in the diegesis and the audience of a skein of action or thought not foregrounded in the diegesis. Sara's passion, regarded as such only by her students, is accentuated through the role of Frankie. Consequently, the doubling motif, a staple in some early silent Expressionist films, works to reveal Sara to herself and others, including the audience.

The motif of the double, widely used to depict the thematic of the modernist split self in early films such as Max Mack's *The Other* (1913), generally touches on male existential dilemmas. The early *The Student of Prague* (dir. Rye, 1913), featuring the male double, reveals that the subject of the film itself is metaphysical. Further, the male double in this film is reduced to nothingness, marking the inviolate integrity, the sovereign autonomy of the male subject that was threatened. From having an identity as a seeker of knowledge, the student loses himself so entirely that he cannot physically see himself in a mirror, thus erasing all connections to the substantial. For the female, doubling is not so much a matter of despair as it is of extending the boundaries of the self. In an early Asta Nielsen film, *The Abyss* (dir. Gad, 1910), the double affords the middle-class woman sexuality, freedom, and access to modernity. Sara's double in the student project film carries the same powerful surge towards a more complicated identity. Where these early films did not actually allow any reconciliation of the doubles, it is patent that doubling in *Losing Ground* does allow the protagonist to be herself and to move beyond herself. Possessed, in a manner, but by an other that is welcome. Although the plot problem, or the relationship problem between husband and wife, is not resolved, the film does point to some new directions in which to think of the notion of ecstasy for women.

The inclusion of universalism as an important component in black thought, and the definition of black female intellectualism expand the genres of the european and African American essai films alike.

Notes

1   Victor is the name of the oldest brother in *Cruz Brothers* and the name of Sara's husband in *Losing Ground*. The name's connotations are apparent.
2   Kilpeläinen (2012) uses this term to discuss Baldwin's later work; I have borrowed the term "postcategorical" but not followed Kilpeläinen in her suggestion that identity categories would "dissolve."

3
Ambiguities of auteurship

The auteur theory, popular in the late 1980s despite male poststructural demurrals, was repressed, and resurfaced in the early 2000s. Theories of auteurship remain important for filmic traditions outside the mainstream industries, and for women. Indeed, many new studies attempt to situate auteurs within an international frame; however, black filmmakers have had reservations about the traditional model. Derived from two sources, one literary, the other filmic, the institutional definition for classical male film auteurship focuses on the proprietary control of the director over the object of art. Since D. W. Griffith's efforts to legitimize film, film has engaged in several conscious and unconscious efforts to integrate, incorporate, and invalidate its older, more prestigious, rival sister, literature (Peucker 1995). The other source derives from Truffaut's rallying cry against the metteurs-en-scène of French cinema who, he claimed, did not appreciate the true versatility of the filmic medium but inevitably made it subservient to the dramatic arts. He himself was deeply enamored of American film, particularly the legendary Alfred Hitchcock with his insistent cameo appearances, which literalized the auteurial gesture in film and established legal "ownership" over a series of films (Silverman 1992). Membership of the auteurial club was confined to those whose aesthetic style was recognized, as in literary texts, across a body of work. The high masculine definition effectively blocked many women and all minorities from entrance into this exclusive club.

Alternate models of auteurship

African American critics are ambiguous about the value of an auteur-driven cinema. Although some critics welcomed the films of the LA School for integrating the black vernacular and the blues aesthetic in their work, others questioned the newfound respect granted to these films in restricted art and university circles: "But does not that limited success mask and cushion the lack of success in its stated aim—to reach the black community in ways that advance self-definition through cinematic self-examination?" (Taylor 1995: 434). The fear is that the films do not speak to wider black audiences and remain "curiosities." However, yet others believe that such criticism becomes an implicit demand that black films fit into the Hollywood paradigm, which, they justly claim, would only appropriate the black vernacular to its own ends as Blaxploitation films had done, following Melvin Van Peebles's *Sweet Sweetback's Baadasssss Song* (Francis 2007). Notwithstanding divergent opinions, it is clear that both the LA Independents and the New York Black Independents produced a body of films that belong to the auteur tradition that stretches back to the work of Oscar Micheaux of the silent era.

Feminist film critics have fairly consistently placed a premium on auteurship, starting with key texts on Dorothy Arzner in the 1980s to theorize "counter-cinema," and then developing institutional approaches to women's filmmaking as with Margarethe Von Trotta and other German women filmmakers. Drawing from, but departing from, the stylistic centering of feminist auteur studies, critics in the 2000s have maintained that feminist auteurship revolves around the film's ideological establishment of the authority of the female. Many of these analyses focused on the manner in which feminist film was successful in subverting the male gaze produced by a masculine cinematic apparatus. Trajectories of looking have received less attention from black feminist critics, who have directed us to a white national imaginary that renders black women invisible, or that reinscribes white male fantasies of black women on screen.

Dominant feminist theories about the male gaze do not obtain as black female directors like Dash, Chadha, Cheryl Dunye, and Amma Asante suggest that black female invisibility on screen, the default mode when they are not fetishized, denies black women femininity (Ramanathan 2006: 45–77). While these ideas have been circulating among black cultural critics, mainstream feminist theorization excludes these considerations, ultimately equating the term "women" with european american women (Hollinger 2012: 230–47). Dishearteningly, despite the writings on international women's film and third world women's film, none of the international/comparative/third world critics figure, as do very few directors, obscuring the long history of women's independent filmmaking, and defining "women's film" and their auteurship in routine terms that sidestep the possibility of more inclusive definitions of women's film and auteurship (Badley et al. 2016: 1–23).

The inclusion of Collins's work in a feminist genealogy of films encourages us to reconsider the very real importance of women's visibility, in this instance black women's visibility in the public space outside the routing of the male (white) gaze. Collins returns to the literary and integrates the philosophical to confer both authority and visibility in the diegesis on her black and minority characters.

Paradoxically, while not fitting into models of male film auteurship, Collins does have some kinship with the earliest notion of auteurship, propounded by Alexandre Astruc, of the "caméra-stylo." Instances of writing in a filmic text are powerful indications of the auteur's insignia (Fischer 2013). *Losing Ground*'s opening features the protagonist writing on the whiteboard, and later she is seen typing an essay. Although such writing seems to insert the proprietary right of the director, like the post-structuralists, Collins was acutely aware of the linguistic discursive, particularly in the making of a film. Consequently, for her, the text would not be attached exclusively to a private vision of the director. A feminist film theorization on auteurship rests on Collins's universalist world view and her registration of the authority of minority and black subjects in the diegesis.

For women directors, as mentioned earlier, the self-fashioning of the female subject in the diegesis was a route to establishing female auteurship. Black film directors, preoccupied with the national cultural imaginary of the black community, had to find a route to universalism that did not center the individual subject. Philosophically, there was no precedent for the black individual's experience to have universal relevance, as distinct from white subjects for whom this was normative. Thus, although white women may have been excluded from the normative universal, their access to it in film was not blocked by a massif of blankness as was the case with black subjects with reference to visuality. As African Americans in film do not have the prerogative of "white looking power," and were denied visibility and presence in film, the introduction of the *idea* of black self-representation on screen was imperative, trumping traditional proprietary gestures. Thus, while european american filmmakers and black filmmakers confront comparable dilemmas, the specificity of race in the visual scene renders the trope of multiple black self-representations crucial to the registration of authority in the visual field. Like other black filmmakers, such as Lee and Gunn, Collins introduces characters who represent themselves; moreover, she develops an expanded debate on self-representation in her films.

Collins does not settle on a single surrogate who would serve as a substitute but distributes the surrogate function liberally, limiting the traditional authority of the auteur but expanding that of a range of characters through their access to self-representation or authorship of various kinds. In her writings and in her films, Collins's auteurial signature is manifest by way of both male and female auteurial surrogates. She combines the use of the literary, the visual, *and* the techniques of film to amplify their authority partly by expressing their reflectiveness on how they inhabit space, how they live in time, and how they understand and work with language to know themselves.

Themes of the artist, her/his interiority, and her/his desire pervade all of her work. Both her films feature portraits of artists as do all her writings. In a very real sense, Collins is very much in search of the forms of creativity that Alice Walker suggests are so important to grasping the complex everyday continuity of black women's creativity in their communities. Walker explores the notion of what the creative process might have been like without the stockpile of amplified male, and the more restricted euroamerican female, literary tradition. In a deliberate move, she strikes out Virginia Woolf's questions about how a sixteenth-century British woman of talent must have felt to substitute how a woman ("born or made a slave") would feel (Walker 1983: 231–43). Dunye later was to reflect on this theme with regard to film in *Watermelon Woman* (1996). Collins responds to the question of specificity in tradition, whether literary or cinematic, by emphasizing the universal of the outsider expressing oneself, regardless of the form. For Collins, the language of the story bridged all art forms. And in direct response to Walker's question of how a talented woman of slave extraction might feel, she features a range of creative forms in her work. Like Walker, she insistently registers the creativity and the authority that each of her characters has, a function of her belief in multiple forms of creative expression. Collins's ability to excavate the imaginations of her characters ensures a genealogical connection in the black community, brought to the fore by the actors and their own glimpses of history. And film for her was about using language to articulate these imaginings as an author might, if with materials other than pen and paper (Collins 1984a; Nicholson 1988/9).

Invested in bringing the linguistic richness of literature to film, Collins sought to incorporate diverse idioms in her films. Collins herself stresses that she is a craftsperson, and that as a skilled editor of many years and a film instructor for seven years, she wanted to acquire a "language" to be able to tell stories with a twist. She specifically chooses the Roth story because of its appeal but almost more so because of its distance from her own life and her writing (Franklin 1981: 31).

Collins was known for encouraging her actors to improvise. In translating a story from Henry Roth's *The Cruz Chronicle* to the screen, Collins worked with José Machado to reshape the character and gestures of Felipe, the brother most reluctant to work for the eccentric Miss Malloy in *The Cruz Brothers and Miss Malloy*. In this film, an older, wealthy, New York woman enlists the young Cruz brothers to restore her house to its former glory, offering them a fantastic salary. Felipe is suspicious, and unlike his characterization in the Roth story where he is largely a stupefied brute, here he is funny in his chagrin, and physically plastic, showing a vulnerability that is not patent in the Roth short story. Collins maintained that she relied on professional actors to follow through with action and character cues, thus involving them in lending texture to the "vision" of the film. This would seem to be as distant from any claims of auteurship as possible, and indeed a canceling of it. The two principles that guide her work are at the crux of the auteur motif: her insistence on language, and her conviction that she needed to do stories whereby no one was "manipulated" (Collins [1980] 2015). Her narrative design then is based on allowing characters to tell their own stories, a series of linked focalizations attesting to the universal relevance of each story. Collins avoids omniscient narration, and devises strategies that would enable the subjects to play a part in telling their stories. The language and techniques used to narrate the stories are inevitably "manipulated" but the characters are not. Author/artist figures litter her films demanding that the viewer scrutinize the transparency of the narration to ascertain whether story and character are slanted. That the artist figure is central in all her texts attests to the importance of insider/self-representation in the telling of black/minority narratives, a priority, given the skewed nature of the cultural repository of blackness.

Narrative authority

The trope of ownership over representation occurs in other black independent film, including Spike Lee's later *Joe's Bed-Stuy Barbershop* (1983). Houston Baker argues that despite the young black photographer's understanding that blacks should control their own images, he participates in an economy of white desire whereby his photography of a black female calendar model articulates a secondary desire, responding to a primary white desire for black bodies as coin. The photographer's artistic creation is, to some extent, a cannibalization of the self at the cost of the female, feeding white desire (Baker Jr. 1993: 154–77). The commodification of black narratives, their production for other (white) desires, is actively contested by Victor's investment in recording his life for himself, a valuation of the self in *The Cruz Brothers*. Sara in *Losing Ground* embarks on several creative projects that are responsive to her desire for fulfillment as an intellectual and a human being. A philosopher critic, she is entrusted with interpreting bodies of knowledge for the next generation, ensuring the continuation of the species as thinkers. Her research on ecstasy is to find out if she can experience extreme states, and to nourish herself. And when she acts in the student's film, it is to seek out different dimensions for herself.

Feminist film has flirted with the trope of the female artist; for example, Julie Taymor's *Frida* (2002) and Agnès Merlet's *Artemisia* (1998), but the abstract premise at the center of Collins's two narrative films is unusual in its location of creativity as authority in film.

African American film too has made serious gestures towards the black subject as scientific intellectual in *Ganja and Hess* (dir. Gunn, 1973), and as everyday philosopher in *Killer of Sheep* (dir. Burnett, 1977). Granting that the subjects in the films actively refrain from fitting into a received cultural placement, the space itself is continuous, making it difficult to void the unequal relationship of blacks to the dominant spaces of the white world. The reflections of the subjects are likewise burdened by the weight of the knowledge that free thinking is itself time stolen. In *The Cruz Brothers*, that dis-ease in space is totally absent; instead, we encounter the imperceptible feeling of ease when the Cruz brothers dance, wobble, and run across a trip wire on the bridge, playing, rather than performing. The sequence, while seemingly realistic, conjures up what Alejo Carpentier in the

1920s described as the marvelous real of the Americas that unlike surrealism, or expressionism, was ontologically real but could occur only in this new world (Carpentier 2006). In the sequence where the brothers highstep it across the trip wire, with only the sky above them and the lush greenery of upstate New York around them, their lives are imbued by a rare, isolated magic, almost as though they were the first to be here. Shades of Macondo in New York State. Henry Roth, the author of *The Cruz Chronicle* that the film is based on, wished very much to do "an American version of a Hundred Years of Solitude" (Roth commentary in Collins [1980] 2015). Many of the stories in the collection skirmish with unusual or inexplicable occurrences; the film fleshes out a single story in a sustained, and North American, magical realist mode. Locating black/minority subjects in this world that is not exclusively bound to white authority enables Collins to establish black/minority intellectual authority in film.

The opening sequence of *Cruz Brothers* illustrates this auteurial combination of the family romance of magical realism, insider narration in an epic frame. The voice over of the narrator is unnamed, but it is implied that it could be the ghost father of young Victor, who very deliberately records his impressions of the town. When the film opens, it appears that the male voice over narrator will ultimately exert a certain magisterial authority over the narrative, almost as though it were a chronicle foretold, but such is not the case, showing how Collins works with the mode of magical realism but with the intent of leaving possibilities open. In the urtext of magical realism, Gabriel García Márquez's *One Hundred Years of Solitude*, the last of the Buendía family reads of their life as told by Melquíades, written in the sacred language of Sanskrit. In contrast, in the film, the father/ghost, the ancestral presence, which is a recurring feature of the collective auteurship of black women, is ineffectual here, providing a counterpoint from which to read Victor's own creative enterprise of recording his thoughts in a little machine (Ryan 2005). In a mise-en-cadre, shortly after Victor and his two brothers have returned home, we see Victor handling the tape and talking to "Poppa." Victor, whom Poppa calls the "family historian," uses the tape machine as an auditory record that subtly lends *Cruz Brothers* the diary film dimension. Indeed, the machine and the tapes, predating the cassette format, appear to hold the sheer joy of the discovery of ice in the opening of *One Hundred Years*. Victor's taping process also recalls the arcane secrecy practiced in Colonel Aureliano Buendía's private laboratory where he retreated to explore the mysteries of science. In her commentary after the screening of the film, Collins said that she was "toying with myth/fantasy; illusion/truth" (Collins [1980] 2015). A wry moment in the film when Victor tries to prise all these apart in a humorous challenge to himself and to us is when he holds the dinky tape recorder out to Poppa and asks him to speak into it, raising the question of whether Poppa's ghostly voice can leave material traces. Through much of the film, Victor carries the authority of the player on stage who holds the audience in his grip with his soliloquies because, of course, we only hear Poppa, we never see him. Victor's conversations with Poppa and into the tape recorder then show only him in the frame, leaving him with a grip over the narrative, even as he is extremely vulnerable as he reveals himself to his tape recorder and struggles with the family ghost who tries to curb his adventures. Poppa is not as culpable as José Arcadio Buendía, the patriarch of the Buendía family, but he certainly leaves the brothers in the lurch when he is shot during a botched bank heist. And while the Cruz brothers start out with a bungled hotwiring attempt, thanks to Victor's ability to communicate with people outside the Puerto Rican community, they move outside their own narrow territory.

The opening sequence also shows how Collins insists on her subjects having some control over their space. In feminist film, one of the key visual breakthroughs occurs when we begin to see female protagonists not confined to certain domestic spaces but taking command over the open spaces. A classical case in point is Dorothy Arzner's *Christopher Strong* (1933), which shows a trouser wearing Katharine Hepburn blazing her way through the city in a motorbike, striding across open ground, and ultimately swallowing up miles in the sky during her around-the-world flight.

Collins shows Victor's measurement of the spaces around him in a manner that interposes his perspective of the town, pre-empting any suggestion of trepidation about access to the space. As Victor speaks of the town in amused tones, with more than a slight tinge of irony about its whiteness and shabbiness, various street scenes are interspersed, authenticating his running commentary. A wavy tracking shot of the camera moving from right to left while the cars move in the other direction in semi-darkness appears to catch the quality of a mysterious town with no inhabitants but plenty of cars to hotwire. Victor exceeds the remit of the family historian and doubles as a town archivist.

Auteurial surrogates

In *Cruz Brothers*, family history is a route to affirming identity. José, the dreamy brother, says, "We got no records," whereupon Felipe, cast as the more unaware brother, says they have plenty, by which he means that they have plenty of long playing records. That two of the brothers know the value of keeping track of family history, are self-conscious about being part of something larger, and that their stories have value shows that they are what Gramsci might call organic intellectuals, and more importantly, that they have the desire to express themselves artistically in what Minh-ha might dub art for everyday use (Gramsci 1971; Minh-ha 1991).

An aura of transcendence marks the second sequence of the film that introduces us to Victor's archival project. The scene resists classical transparent realism and turns to an engaged modernism, perspectival but valid through its investment in the mythical character of Victor and the truth value of his narrative. Both Roth and Collins thought there was something mythical about the Cruz brothers and their exploits that seemed to put them in a different world (Collins [1980] 2015).[1] The film seeks to understand their place and their displacement in the culture through a rendition of their exploits. The Roth stories attempt to mark the differences between the Cruz brothers and the others in the Puerto Rican community by using realistic language to describe the community while presenting the brothers as mythical. Where the Cruz brothers are mythical characters in the Roth stories, in the film their presence renders the world magical, in part because the film does not allow them to be compared with other Puerto Rican men. The only two "characters" the brothers encounter could both be considered ghosts: "Poppa," and Miss Malloy, whose entrance and role in their lives is more than slightly incredible. Poppa flatly states that only Victor, as the oldest, has the privilege of being able to see him. Victor is further "gifted" or "burdened" by his self-appointed task as historian. As he dryly comments, his brothers are enjoying pinball machine games while he, "the lucky brother," is talking to the machine.

Our first view of Victor on his own is shot to create an effect that is whimsical and slightly mythical in that he appears to be perched high up, giving him some sweep over the terrain. The camera tracks and pauses, and then cuts to the window; the exterior

Figure 3.1 *Cruz Brothers*: The ethnographer

edging of the window in an exact reproduction of the frame of a painting. Victor is in his room with his head in the center of the window/painting frame, partly occupied with Poppa, and partly with the tape recorder, a Janus-like character, who cuts himself to size with his self-mockery.

When the brothers meet Miss Malloy, a woman from a different world, and a different time, which is almost as important as being from a different race, José is the brother who most picks up on her cadences of the past. Her ruminations are poetic, as she peels layers from herself to find another self that she vaguely hopes exists, and so like José, despite many material artefacts, she appears to have no records of the self. She, more than the brothers, explicitly has a vision of restoring the house to its original splendor, an artist summoning up her past, refashioning herself. The project subtly impinges on shaping the Cruz brothers, a seemingly tangential but willed choice on her part. When she first accosts the brothers, she is presented in an impressionistic mode, in the guise of one

Figure 3.2 *Cruz Brothers*: The figure of fate?

of the Three Fates, perhaps even as Lachesis, the sister who measures the thread of life. Miss Malloy has the measure of the Cruz brothers when she says that "they tempt the Fates," an adroit use of language that hints at her attraction for them, but unlike the mythological Fate Lachesis, she is measuring out her own life, and hence does not cast the shadow of an intractable fate on the Cruz brothers. Their coming into her life removes the fated quality of her own.

The quality of Miss Malloy's staged speech brings with it the illusory quality of a performance. Miss Malloy herself would seem to be directing a stage play, one in which she plays the leading role, the Cruz brothers being her "young princes." There is more than a glimmer of the stage director in her aspiration to create the perfect mise-en-scène for her exit lines by stage managing the restoration of the grounds and the house. In that sense, she serves as a surrogate auteurial figure, as does Victor the archivist.

José, more than Victor, is spellbound by Miss Malloy and the setting of her house, telling her enthusiastically that it could be in a "movie." And soon enough, he who had bemoaned the lack of "records" of their memories wants to buy a camera. In José, we witness the struggle of the performer who breaks away from the director, touchingly wanting to perform the prescribed role, and yet fearing that it is taking him away from his reality. In other words, he refuses to be manipulated by the "author," reminding us of Luigi Pirandello's characters who even as they search for an author restrict his authority. That he succeeds in buying the camera and in taking pictures countervails his role as performer in Miss Malloy's improvisational theatre.

Two sequences, one in the middle of the film, when José is still wonderstruck by Miss Malloy's house, and one later, in the ballroom, illustrate this conflict. A low angle shot shows José nestled up on a tree branch in greenery that can only be described as sylvan. A long shot from José's perspective captures Miss Malloy wearing a broad-brimmed, stylish hat walking towards the tree. He strikes a pose for his admiring fan, hamming the actor. She asks him for a line; he has no line, but when pressed comes up with "I'd like to take a picture of you, Miss Malloy." She is enchanted, but he has switched roles neatly: he is no longer the actor in her artistic direction, she is the actor in his. In a sly nod to Lorenzo Tucker, the "Black Valentino," Collins has Miss Malloy call José "Valentino." Of course, José does not know who Valentino is, so although he wishes to act, he cannot be slotted into established roles. The refusal is starker, if filled with anguish, later when he is dancing with her. A long shot presents them in almost ethereal lighting, but the secret spell is shattered for the audience who glimpse Felipe spying on them. We cut to a close-up of José's face, crumpled, saying that this is "crazy," confirming José's conflicted feelings as actor in Miss Malloy's theatre. When Miss Malloy pleads with him, he desperately asks her to stop. José and Miss Malloy are unaware that the other two brothers are watching spellbound. Yet, our look is not relayed through their gaze; the brothers differ in their reactions, disarraying ours. The scene closes to hushed silence. The effect is similar to the theatrical curtain call.

Felipe, the recalcitrant brother, is a study of confusion in the film. He is totally taken aback by Miss Malloy's association with the Cruz brothers. Increasingly estranged by their willing assimilation into Miss Malloy's world, Felipe appeals to ancestral authority. Always lurking, he sneaks into Victor's room, listens to the tapes that say that Poppa has not been around for a while, and snarls at Victor that he does not like it when Poppa is not around. His fragile authority as the tough one cracks, even as he dimly understands that his brother is on a plane of understanding he cannot quite grasp. While he never completely acquires any authority, he is shown as struggling to understand the concept. He becomes increasingly disturbed by Victor and José's unorthodox closeness to Miss Malloy. He stumbles upon them in an enchanting clearing ground and watches as each brother, with the steady courtesy of an Elizabethan gentleman, dances in step with Miss Malloy. The composition of the scene envelops off-screen space. A long shot introduces Miss Malloy as she dances in the center of the green carefully edged by bushes producing the effect of an interior and an exterior. Victor makes an entrance from stage right, bows, as the camera with a slight waver catches them in the dance. A tracking shot takes us to José entering from stage rear, watching them, and then stepping into the ground, as he takes Victor's place and dances with greater ardor than Victor, with eyes closed; José enjoys the courtly ritual, and the erotic pleasure of the dance. A cut brings us to the sound of clattering as Felipe blusters through the bushes muttering "loca." He reacts with fear, muttering "Poppa, oh Poppa" several times, looking to a higher authority to sort out this outrage. His sense of stability is completely shaken up.

The soundtrack follows Felipe's fears for the stability of his identity. Through the whole sequence, the soundtrack plays plaintive music with no readily visible diegetic source. The effect is shattering when Felipe shouts for the music to stop, a moment of cutting through the magic that he too had experienced but wanted to end. When the music stops, the clash between the improbable and the mundane is jarring. When the dancers pause, shocked, all are aware of the boundaries that had been breached. Although Felipe appears to be outside the magical circle, the scene emphasizes his vulnerability and his visceral struggle with the notion that a Puerto Rican can be something other than what the stereotype dictates.

Philosophy and art in film

Losing Ground is overt about its auteurial surrogate in the diegesis and forceful about establishing black female authority. We start with a medium close-up of Sara mid-stream in a lecture on Sartre and existentialism. A high angle long shot tracks from the top row to the bottom row of students seated in a lecture hall until we get to Sara at the lectern. We see a full shot of her before we see another shot of her from another side of the room. The vastness of the space gives her absolute power of the word; and although not a voice over, the lecture carries the overtones of ex nihilo discourse.

It is clear, too, that the professor is thinking through the problem of existence, what life means, as she explains the precepts of existentialism. Sara speaks with passion about war, existence, the absurd movement, and Sartre's texts making the abstract questions of essence and existence immediate and urgent ones. The terms of the lecture secure the film's place in the genre of philosophical films. From the routine questions at the opening, a conversation between instructor and student shifts to a conversation on Genet and issues of social identity including race and sexuality. If *The Cruz Brothers* validates the organic intellectual, the artist, and the journeyman's fears of the intellectual, *Losing Ground* opens with what Gramsci might term the traditional intellectual. Whereas in Gramscian terms a traditional intellectual consolidates the authority of the ruling class, and in the Althusserian formulation shores up their coerciveness by ideological state apparatuses, invoking consent for their hegemony (Gramsci 1971; Althusser 1971), Sara enthusiastically tells her students about Sartre's book on Genet emphasizing the subversive challenge of the outsider to the status quo:

> It's the finest analysis of being an outsider I've ever read ... it's a wonderful book, he touches every feeling, every mental attitude connected with exclusion.
> *The young man stares at her with deep respect.* (Klotman 1991: 127)

The script and scene alike characterize Sara as an instructor who commands the unqualified respect of her students based on her knowledge and her intellectual energy.

Within the diegesis, Sara, while maintaining the authority of the intellectual, brings a passion into the discourse that militates against the detachment, the lie of objectivity, that traditional philosophy might be expected to purvey.[2] Sara is not only an able communicator of philosophical ideas, she does research in areas that delve into the interior and seeks to name them. In this endeavor, like feminist philosopher Luce Irigaray, she seeks a language to articulate experiences that are transcendent but not necessarily connected to the Judeo-Christian religious tradition. Again, Collins forcefully signals that the film is about philosophy and human beings seeking to find new philosophical frameworks to understand themselves.

Married to an artist who makes plans for the summer that revolve around his painting projects, Sara Rogers insists on having some control over her time to pursue her research on ecstatic experience. In a sequence that gives pride of place to philosophical language, we see Sara reading in a library. The image of her reading, far removed from other images of black women in film, establishes reading as an activity in and of itself. The trope, a carryover from African American literature, is dense in claiming the literacy of black women as an absolute. As she reads, we hear her voice over puzzling out the intricacies of experiences that are "original," unmediated by the divine. The text she reads outlines the idea that as human beings our belonging in society does not vitiate against our "consciousness" being "original." That this deeply felt thought is invaluable for the self is a proposition that Sara will test later when she explores the connections between being for others and being for the self when she performs in her student's film.

In the library, Sara is accosted by a man who regards her with astonishment as she seems to be eating the words and swallowing the ideas. Their discussion ranges from western theological concepts on ecstasy to the Gnostics, who were more "intuitive." Sara is contemplating the flows of disorderly Dionysiac energy. Her conversation with the unnamed stranger, who himself seems to have been summoned for the specific purpose of the discussion, also takes in the possibility of otherworldly realities through psychic readings. Thus, her notions of philosophy are not exclusively derived from the western Enlightenment tradition. Here, we see Sara claiming an authority as a pioneering researcher, one who can contribute to the thought of the world. The combination of the mise-en-scène, with its aura of the sacred, and her own voice over, again ex nihilo, forges a harmonious balance between place and sound, indicating not just Sara's ease with both but her mastery.

The auteurial signature could not be more deliberate. Collins herself was a professor, had translated a monograph on precisely the topic that Sara was discussing, and had written fiction and plays featuring the theme (Mars [1946] 1977). To add to the richness of the character's intellectual orientation, Collins also features her as the lead character in a student film. That metafilmic device is yet another way that the auteurial signature is inscribed in the film, commenting on what film itself can offer philosophy, the dramatization of abstract and pragmatic thought.

The Eisensteinian model—dialectical montage—demands intellectual reasoning, advancing though on the processes of history. In his discussion of Eisenstein's use of dialectical montage and the close-up, Deleuze suggests that the notion of the time-image indicates that film can advance the kinds of questions that animate the study of philosophy, and can perhaps even introduce new ones (Rushton 2012: 101). Collins's departure into existential questions of experience would constitute such a query. She had made an extensive study of these films in France, and we can discern that direction in her films even when the themes are different. The literary references to Albert Camus and the absurd that Godard makes in *Breathless* (1960) through the character of Michel Poiccard are here evoked in a philosophical context. The film features discussions on these themes among Sara, her artist husband, Victor, and Duke, the otherworldly acquaintance Sara meets at the library. As Collins has acknowledged, she particularly admired Rohmer's *My Night with Maud* for being able to choreograph the language of film with that of ideas; a film where all people do is talk, and we watch, riveted. Rohmer's film features long conversations on Pascal (Nicholson 1988/9: 10). To a large extent, Collins found a way of detaching the narrative scaffolding that Rohmer uses to arrive at a sharp skeletal discussion by putting the intellectual question at the center of life's doings, in the sequences of Sara lecturing and of her reading. Thus, Collins's film places the philosophical question as the quest motif, compelling the narrative to follow the arc of the philosophical.

The pragmatist school of thought rejects the idea that film can be properly philosophical, unless it is about the philosophy of film, and here, as Collins's film uses the film within the film to theorize on the philosophical question of ecstasy, *Losing Ground* could be considered exemplary (Smith and Wartenberg 2006). The argument put forth by critics who believe it is an over-reach for films to strive to be philosophy is that film's use value lies in simplifying philosophical concepts and making them more accessible to a wider audience. Certainly, the film could be used as a companion piece to discuss existentialism, its social applications in contexts that Sartre had not anticipated, its relevance to race and to gender.

The motif of the artist further allows us to think through ideas of the self and existence as conventionally represented by philosophers and artists. In many senses, the narrative's overarching conflict is abstract in that it stages a confrontation between a philosophical and an artistic perspective on self and existence. Staged as a debate that has reaches beyond the intellectual, Sara and Victor, her artist husband, talk about the emotions and ideas provoked by practicing philosophy and art. It is tempting to understand this debate in this ultimately philosophical film as being about the differences between the male and female auteurial signatures. The same director who had with infinite delicacy constituted Victor and José in *The Cruz Brothers and Miss Malloy* as auteur surrogates is reticent about the male artist's authority when it is placed alongside the female. Certainly, both the male artist and the female philosopher wish for some relationship with the creative that far exceeds the claims of possession or legal authority, the intellectual roots of the concept of authorship and auteurship (Silverman 1992). And they do have a common understanding that "black" as a signifier is slid to qualify, classify, and perhaps exclude black art and philosophy. That particular bind for scholars and critics continues as they struggle between the dialectic of universality and specificity. The philosopher George Yancy reports that when he told his "white philosopher mentor" that he was thinking of specializing in African American philosophy, the mentor's response was: "Make sure you don't get pegged" (2004: 1). Both Sara and Victor do not lend too much credence to the pegging. While Victor mocks it, and himself, when he says he is a "genuine Negro success," Sara when discussing

Sartre, Genet, and "exclusion" in metaphysical and philosophical terms suggests that the specific *is* universal, and that the universal in turn *is* specific. Of Genet, she says, "He touches every feeling, every attitude connected with exclusion." The specific experience of estrangement, whether of homosexuality, ethnicity, race, or gender, flows from the particular to the universal, while the awareness of absurdity as the only rational response to an arbitrary world flows from the universal to the particular.

Sexuality and the male artist

Philosophical differences between Victor and Sara run through the film, as Victor deliberately undermines Sara's authority by mocking her philosophical project for the summer; her need for books and intellectual stimulation as being less authentic than his own artistic "trance"-like impulses. Collins uses this current of tension between Victor and Sara to explore the differences between male and female auteurship. She deconstructs Victor's authority by showing the texts of the future subjects of his paintings. Although Victor claims that he is shifting to representational art as distinct from abstract art, the point of view shots that capture Victor's subjects show that he is all too invested in inserting himself as auteur in his depiction. As he walks through the town, his sketch pad open, he appears to invite the attention of each of the subjects, all of them being Puerto Rican women. Victor's attempt at his first sketch delicately reveals his desires as an artist and as a man. A low angle slightly slanted shot places Victor almost at the edge of the frame as he glances up at the balcony; a cut takes us to the woman leaning on the balcony sill. Victor then looks up at the woman, smiling gallantly but with gestures that beckon. The woman returns the look, and then turns away almost deliberately posing. This scenario is repeated three times, making the artistic endeavor an erotic transaction between the male artist and the (unwitting) female model.

Ambiguities of auteurship 71

Figure 3.3 *Losing Ground*: "Form, color, light"

Collins contrasts the male artist's relationship to art and sex with the female intellectual's. Their ideas are of course based not on gender but on their intellectual and artistic formations. While gender may not be primary, it inserts itself insidiously into the discourse; thus, the language used is revealing.

After a shoot in New York City, Sara returns to their upstate New York house with her fellow actor, Duke, the gentleman she had met in the library. Even before Sara and Duke arrive, Collins elaborates on the link between sex and painting. When Victor is lobbing back and forth regarding the merits of abstract vs. representational art with his abstract painter friend Carlos, he contrasts Carlos's purity with his own deceit. We had first seen him in the neighborhood, sketching women, jaunty and flirtatious. His acquaintanceship with Celia, a young Puerto Rican woman, starts on a different note. A medium long shot shows us Victor in the background looking at Celia dance in the park. He is carried away by the ebullience of the moment and moves to join her, but not before pointedly throwing his sketch pad in the air. She becomes his model. Cross cutting systematically follows the pursuits of Sara in New York and Victor in upstate. The parallel editing is so symmetrically matched that Collins features Sara dancing in the shooting of the film with Duke, her acquaintance from the library, and Victor slow dancing in an intimate space with Celia. The scenes of Sara and Victor are carefully patterned to enable the viewer to make her/his own judgments.

Sara is presented as very calm and rational in her discussion with her mother on Victor's sexual/artistic adventuring. In a discussion with her mother about her husband's sexual behaviors, the protagonist says without rancor that there have always been women. When her mother asks her quite explicitly how she feels about it, she says that Victor is always having sex with "color, form, light." And it appears that she is admiring his capacity to do the latter. What is striking is not the distinction between the women and sex, and painting and sex, but the similarity between the two. At this juncture, Sara has just started acting in a student's film project and is beginning to feel ambivalent about Victor's enthusiasm for his latest painting subject, Celia, the young Puerto Rican woman.

We see a petulant Victor in the company of Celia and Carlos, his friend who is an abstract painter. When Sara and Duke join them, he demands attention from Celia and brusquely dismisses Sara with, "I keep forgetting you don't know how to dance." The irony is not lost on the viewer; despite Sara's demurrals, we have seen, not one, but two dance sequences that the diegetic audience applauded. The evening and morning after take a nasty turn when Victor, playful but ugly, insists on getting into Celia's sleeping bag and pushes himself on top of her. Sara comes into the scene and is appalled at what she sees. Curiously, the issue of Victor's piling on to Celia is disregarded, as this scene becomes a part of not only Sara's marital relationship with Victor but their distinct approaches to art and the intellect. Her spontaneous fury with Victor's behavior is all the more explosive because of her even, temperate speech throughout. Given the horror and shame of the moment, Sara's

Figure 3.4 *Losing Ground*: "Don't you take your dick out like it was artistic like it's some goddamn paintbrush"

response about Victor's artistic/sexual being is both philosophical and analytic: "Don't you take your dick out like it was artistic like it's some goddamn paintbrush?" Victor's angry response is almost unbelievable, seemingly claiming the droit de l'artiste.

The opening sequences of the film subtly draw out the differences between a possible male and female auteur surrogate figure in the diegesis. While Sara is in the pit of the lecture hall and her students are higher up visually, the power of her attempting to think things through with them to some extent and to communicate *with* them makes it a very dialogic interaction, even if she is the cardinal authority figure in the room. Before we first see Victor, we hear him off screen talking to Sara, and when we do first see him, we see him from Sara's point of view. Victor is up on a ladder, leaning down towards her, while she looks up at him; she resists climbing it, but eventually succumbs. In and of itself, the sequence does not suggest any kind of domination, but followed up as it is intermittently in the narrative by at least four sequences, two with Sara and two with Celia, where he is standing and painting the female model, who in each case seems to be openly resentful about the stillness forced on her, the scenes together suggest a model of male authoritarianism and artistry over female inertness and matter.

The deconstruction of the male artist, a substitute for the male auteur, is very specific and directed at auteurial investment in the signature as opposed to the work of art. Victor begins with a yearning for "purity" in art, abstract art that would express what his mentor calls "form." He has a light-hearted conversation with Sara about the differences in his attitudes to abstract and representational art. Intriguingly, we enter their conversation mid-stream. A medium long shot frames Sara posing in a stylized way, seated by the window. They are chatting as Victor paints her:

> Victor.   ...too representational...
> Sara.   What do you mean...
> Victor.   I've shied away from it as too easy...
> Sara.   You mean to paint people and things is a cop-out.

Although mocking, Sara gets to the truth when she implies that Victor would have to pay attention to the subject in representational matter, unlike abstract art where he would be focusing on shape and color. Representing people, Sara insinuates, takes looking into their truth, not putting the artistic imprimatur on canvas. Sara herself appears to define her intellectual interests in both abstract and concrete dimensions. The connection she makes between Genet's existentialism, his outsider status, and its social relevance resonates with Angela Davis's notion that philosophy is not merely a "specific mode of thought" as much as it is a "quotidian way of living in the world" (Yancy 1998: 7). The protagonist in *Losing Ground* might well agree but add that reconciling the external and the internal would constitute a philosophical way of life, a common thread in black philosophy, African diaspora thought, and Eastern philosophy, but not quite so central in the euro-american philosophical tradition.

Figure 3.5 *Losing Ground*: Male artist/auteur

The authority of the actor

If Victor's authority is deconstructed, in an unexpected twist, Sara's is too. The collected persona of the opening sequence is slowly altered by the pulls of the people surrounding her. While Victor's high-handed suggestion that Sara move upstate for the summer, follow him and sideline her own research project, is overtly patronizing, Sara's mother's suggestion is no less an affront but perhaps less noticeable. When Sara, impassioned, describes the state she experiences when she knows she has understood something deeply about the world, in other words, created a relevant philosophy, her mother suggests that she write a play about her mother's life. The moment is softened by the humor; the irony, however, is that Sara herself finds a different kind of philosophy through her mother's chosen passion, acting.

The motif of acting is doubled in the film with the mother playing a theatre actor, and the daughter acting in a film. The female "actor" in the film within the film carries the "trace" or the Derridean sense of radical otherness from the unitary subject (Derrida 1976).[3] The actor is very often the most dominated person on the set, but can frequently, especially in the feminist and African American film context, transmit a social authority far exceeding her diegetic role. In many instances, this authority directly refers to the accrual of greater agency in the social. Lena Horne in 1930s and 40s Hollywood films played herself in set musical cabaret pieces. Her presence in the film invited a more socially inflected reading. Her persona registered the entrance of black women even as the diegesis of the film sought to constrain her to her acting role (Ramanathan 2015). Rather, her popularity commanded a public space for black women. Mrs. Rogers the theatre actor, and Sara Rogers the star of a film directed by a student would seem to express this double articulation of the black female actor, disempowered and empowered.

Mrs. Rogers complains about the typecast mammy roles she is obliged to keep playing. She quips that she is expected to be thinking of God, but spends more time thinking about men! The stereotypical role that Sara seems to be playing in the student film, replete with performance elements, is close enough to the role of the Jezebel. In foregrounding these obvious stereotypes, Collins uses a strategy that would later become very useful in feminist films such as Chadha's *Bhaji on the Beach* (1993) where the extra-diegetic interprets the diegesis, mocking its own overblown stereotyping. The contrast between the black archetypes and the persons themselves could not be greater. The disjuncture in the structure between the diegetic and the extra-diegetic renders the auteurial signature shaky. Collins, unlike Chadha later, does not mark the difference decisively but would seem to suggest that even as the archetype is inauthentic, its appearance is belied by the possibility of an emotional truth or authenticity that is paradoxically obscured by the falseness of the appearance. Caryl Phillips's novel on Bert Williams, a stage actor in the 1920s who eventually became one of the most famous actors of his time, delves into the psychic tremors caused by a black man donning blackface and playing a coon. *Dancing in the Dark* (2005) reveals that Bert Williams chooses to use the authority of the entertainer to remind himself and his audience of who he is in the US. Tragedy perhaps, but not pathos. The discrepancies in *Losing Ground* between the archetypal performer, the extra-diegetic dancer and the philosopher professor are pronounced, but the female actor appears to accrue authority in the extra-diegetic sequence which spills over into the diegesis.

The first sequence of the Frankie and Johnny film merely set up the roles of the vaudeville performers featured in the African American folktale to add a theatrical dimension to the film within the film. The vaudeville performer or the theatrical actor can appeal directly to the audience, perhaps even adjusting movements, facial gestures, and line delivery based on the audience response. The Frankie and Johnny sequences combine some elements of stage and film acting to enhance the authority of Frankie, the stage actor, and Sara, the film actor playing the role of stage actor. Performances featuring female figures in film inevitably address the male viewer, suturing his look to that of the male viewer in the diegesis, rendering the female and her emotions secondary to male viewing pleasure.

The Frankie and Johnny sequences overturn the male viewer's expectations, augmenting the authority of the female actor. The second shoot, however, includes Victor in the audience. He is on the edge of the frame, watching in sheer amazement as close-ups on Sara highlight the intense emotions of the stage actor's despair at Johnny's betrayal. When she blows Johnny away with her gun, Victor, placed in the diegesis outside the film within the film, feels physically assaulted. Sara does not return his look.

The acting in the film takes recourse to the centrality of the action and does not engage in manipulation through techniques of cutting or tracking, with the camera holding still to capture the stage performance. The viewer Victor, however, occupies the place of the cinematic viewer. Where cabaret sequences favor frontal shots of female dancers who are on their own, as in Von Sternberg's *The Blue Angel* (1930), and the female performer and male viewer are both part of the diegesis, subtly intimating the power of the male viewer outside the diegesis, here the male viewer is completely on the other side of the screen in the anonymous darkness, lost in the shadows with no role to play but to watch. A very different role for Victor, who cannot abide not being the center of attention. Sara's acting is clearly intended to show the sweep of her imaginative identification with Frankie, but also to expose the tiny gap between the actor and the character she plays, acting Frankie but also her own existence. Differently from the Method style of acting, or the Stanislavskian where the actor is subsumed, here she affirms her presence. And she maintains her authority while devastated. Is she aware that Victor is watching her? This question is pertinent because her sense of herself apart from him, as a creative individual, is crucial to the accrual of feminist authority in the text. Early in the film and through her lectures, both male and female students comment on her passion and her enthusiasm, always politely saying that her husband must appreciate her for what they perceive to be rare qualities. Each time, Sara is perplexed and slightly annoyed. Are these qualities striking because they add to her value in a man's eyes, or are they intrinsically important for her own existence? One critic insists that the comments of the students are an acknowledgment of the teacher's erotic energy; regardless, the female intellectual is placed in the male libidinal frame of reference. That he does not know her, as his startled facial expressions show, points to her graceful departure from established patterns. More emphatically, even though he is looking at her, he does not know her; thus, Collins denies the male the power of vision and, with it, Victor's very identity as a painter, based as it is on vision.

The doubling apparent in the role of the actor/professor, while incongruous, offers a particularly feminist motif in the notion of the inhabitation of otherness that is originally introduced as a topic in the philosophy lecture hall pertaining to existentialism and Genet. The self is represented not in terms of its absolute ego, not as unitary, but doubled. It has become commonplace in feminist criticism to suggest that certain texts approximate l'écriture feminine. While I am not applying that model to this text, I do find the Irirgarayan concept outlined in "When our lips speak together" (without forcing the body homology) quite apt in the doubling of the actor/philosopher: "Not one without the other" referring to completion as a function of doubleness. The "one-sidedness" that Victor had mocked in Sara, the discursive control that Sara wields as an intellectual, is complemented by her acting as an/other seemingly wholly different from her (Irigaray 1985b).

The possibility of the protagonist acting is mentioned early in the film when a student asks, without any hope of being entertained, whether there is any chance of Sara acting in his senior project. She laughs the question away, but later, when Victor dismisses her philosophy research project for the summer, and appears to be in an "ecstatic private trance," she says, almost rebelliously, "I could be another Dorothy Dandridge ..." and then off screen says, "... come to grips with a certain fullness." The language Sara uses to describe Victor, and her comparison of him to a musician who plays his instrument through the day, is almost a projection of what Sara herself is trying to study, ecstasy. *Webster's* most restrictive definition fits the case here: "Implies a trance like state where the mind is fixed on what it contemplates or conceives." The word "trance" is folded into Sara's earlier charge that Victor's "private" ecstasy connotes absence, or "being beside oneself." It is not incidental that in this critique of Victor on a topic she has been researching, she appears, unwittingly, to have found how unsatisfactory some western philosophical disquisitions are. Spontaneously, she offers another model of not "being away" but "being there," using Dorothy Dandridge, the black film actor, almost as a conduit.

It is not accidental that Dandridge is introduced as a response to Victor's artistic (self-)absorption. Collins interjects the notion of authentic artistry by using the figure of the actor. In setting Dandridge up as an ego ideal, Collins obliquely gestures to her place in African American film. Dandridge plays the role of a free-spirited young woman in *Carmen Jones* but is doomed to the fate of the tragic mulatta. The theme of the tragic female mulatta is mentioned in *Losing Ground* at least twice, once with reference to *The Scar of Shame* suggesting that art including the social, or "messy" lives of people, is both valid and extremely vital. Hence Sara's scornful dismissal of Victor when he moots the idea that her desire is spurred by her mother's professional career as an actor.

An early silent film, *The Scar of Shame* (dir. Perugini and produced by Philadelphia Colored Players, 1927) serves as sub-text to the acting motif and throws light on the artistry of the actor. Lucia Lynn Moses plays the role of Louise, a young mulatto female in the city, abused and exploited by her step-father, his friend, and later relegated to a side by her, again not coincidentally, her artist husband, the pianist, seeking to be the black Beethoven. In a more sidereal manner, it adds heft to the idea of the female actor as central to the film, taking us away from the official auteurial signature. That women actors are central to film would seem to be self-evident; however, their importance has largely been understood in terms of the visual pleasure, voyeuristic, scopophilic, fetishistic that they offer. A different strain of feminist scholarship would indicate, particularly in the case of silent cinema, that far from being the objects of manipulation as in the exemplary case of the master auteur, Hitchcock, they are responsible for shaping the character, particularly in instances where scripts were rough, sketchy, and hazy at best. This is true of Lucia Lynn Moses, who carries the film from its beginning when she plays the young girl overwhelmed by the males in her life, themselves beset by the vices of the city. It also speaks to the contributions that Seret Scott, who plays Sara Rogers, brings to the film. Collins and she were close friends, and Scott had acted in many of Collins's plays. In keeping with Collins's approach to filmmaking, Scott did much to act the role of Sara Rogers subtly (Stallings 2011: 52).

To return to the sub-text of the tragic mulatta as it pertains to *Losing Ground*: both the student director, and Duke, Sara's opposite lead in the student film, mention the theme with reference to the African American Frankie and Johnny tale/ballad. The tragic mulatto theme adds to the density of the literariness of the film, without crediting a specific authority, the tale being common property and having a long history in African American women's literature beginning with one of the first novels, Frances Harper's *Iola Leroy*. These intersect with the story of Louise in *The Scar of Shame* and the new black migration to the north. Finding that her upper-caste husband refuses to take her home to his mother and their "set," Louise avenges herself on him by wrongly claiming that he had shot her. She then refashions herself as a city highflyer, but eventually, remorseful, commits suicide. Frankie's blowing Johnny away at the end of the film within the film, with its implications for Sara and Victor, is a reprisal of that theme, insisting on its continued relevance to the African American community, particularly the new post-caste lines that had emerged. When Sara decides to play that role, she also chooses the many others that are imbricated in it, claiming her authority as both philosopher and female actor/artist. That the genealogy of the film stretches to the folkloric, the literary, and the filmic also succeeds in diminishing the controlling command of the conventional director/auteur.

In focusing on the authority of the actor, Collins deliberately moves away from that of the director on set, and instead captures the collaboration of the director, artists, and actors on set to dispense with the singular auteurial signature.

Notes

1 Very, very loosely based on some students who participated in Roth's wife's art therapy courses, the film enlarges their daredevil antics that are plausible and say something larger in and about the culture.
2 As of 2016, the percentage of black women instructors across the ranks is 3 percent (IES: National Center for Educational Statistics, available at <https://nces.ed.gov/fastfacts/display.asp?id=61>, last accessed July 19, 2019). Safe to say, then, that representing a black woman as a "traditional" academic in 1981 is in no way traditional in film, bringing in a thematic about black women in authority seldom seen on screen and still not realized in the work of contemporary filmmakers.
3 In other words, it is only through discourse that we can invoke this presence; the real of the actor is intuited by the trace; the trace does not emerge from the real.

4

The magical marvelous modern

> They would never fall from that narrow railing's grace.
>
> (Roth 1989: 89)

When asked about what she hoped to achieve with her films, Collins chose to speak of the process of filmmaking itself. She said she wrote of characters who would appear grander on screen than they were in real life. She did not want realistic men or women but people with a touch of the mythical about them (Franklin 1981: 31).[1] At first glance, the story of three Puerto Rican boys and a New York woman may not strike us as mythical material. The film's use of "metalanguage" of the magical and the marvelous in a modern context is recognizable to audiences as myth (Sanders 2006: 63). It is useful, for heuristic purposes, to distinguish between the magical and the marvelous in the mythical. The magical is characterized by surface properties that have shock value, the marvelous by a mixing of the real and the extraordinary that is accepted as reality.

Finding the mythical or narrative of Colombia, Márquez's *One Hundred Years of Solitude*, fascinating, Henry Roth transplanted some of the material to North American shores in his *The Cruz Chronicle*. Collins uses a small sliver of this collection of stories of the three brothers to "translate" it into film, to find narrative solutions for the problems of these quasi-mythical characters (Collins [1980] 2015; Klotman [1982] 2015).

Collins identified two problems in the making of the film: firstly, whether to corporealize the ghost father, and secondly, whether Miss Malloy, who is a fairly insubstantial figure in the short story, should take up more narrative space. She decided to use sound to summon the ghost father, and the camera to indicate the origin of the voice very sparingly. These decisions were crucial in the creation of the magical/marvelous aura of *Cruz Brothers*. The film's turn to an alternative mode of realism was prompted by Collins's ideas on the ethical. Her definition of the moral is unorthodox: a "certain friendship" offered by life that enables one, despite social pressures, to develop oneself. The decision to tap into that possibility is, for Collins, a political one. And this means allowing oneself to enjoy experiences, such as the Cruz brothers do with Miss Malloy without being threatened by them. She sought to characterize the Cruz brothers as light-hearted about their own difficulties, and not obsessed with solving them but opening themselves to life (Franklin 1981; Collins [1980] 2015).

Cruz Brothers, although generically similar to Rohmer's essai film *My Night with Maud* (1969), is quite different in terms of both the filmmaking process and the philosophy underlying both films. Rohmer's film follows his short story of the same title. Collins picked one piece in the *Chronicle* called "The Brothers and Miss Malloy," which is only ten pages long. As mentioned earlier, Collins worked closely with the actors to help flesh out the film; thus, it was more of a "translation" than an adaptation.

Rohmer and Collins differ in their conception of grace as they do in the development of the moral in the narrative. *My Night with Maud* suggests that the hero can acquire a predestined grace if he overcomes moral inertia. For Collins, grace is universal and requires only that the individual accept difference in the humanity of others.

Coincidence is integral to the investiture of grace in Rohmer's film, a plot device to drive home the notion of predestination. Although *Cruz Brothers* does have some instances of chance, coincidence does not play a role. The absence of coincidence is vital to the depiction of grace in the film: firstly, because it does not signify the predestination of grace that *My Night with Maud* does, and secondly, because it veers away from African American melodrama's plot machinations, choosing rather to use a magical/marvelous mode of narration where grace is a given.

It is instructive to explore the use of coincidence in *My Night With Maud* and its use as a staple in African American film, with a view to understanding how Collins's mode of narration constructs the universalist world view of the film. Coincidences offer closure in Rohmer's essai film, justice in African American film melodramas.

The plot of *My Night With Maud* is organized around an unnamed male character who comes across as quite morally complacent, revealed in a lengthy conversation that takes up 43 minutes of screen time. His interlocutor is a woman of liberal views, Maud. He sees a girl in church and, seemingly following his fate, marries her. Coincidences litter the film. First, the protagonist meets an old friend while browsing through Pascal; the friend takes him to visit Maud where they discuss Pascal and predestination. Coincidence crops up again when he runs into the girl whom he has seen at church and has decided at first glance to marry. Towards the close of the film, he and his wife separately run into Maud, and here, by another coincidence the protagonist finds out that the adulterous love affair Maud's husband was having was with *his* wife. The Rohmer film needs the last coincidence to establish that the nameless male character chooses to forgive his wife wordlessly and hence acquires grace.

Noting that coincidences in melodrama are particularly apposite to socially subordinated groups, Jane Gaines argues that the complex use of coincidence in melodrama in the African American literary and filmic traditions is essential to obliterate the "narrative 'piling on' of the overwhelming odds against freedom and safety" (1993: 57). Using Micheaux's *Within Our Gates* (1919), she argues that the film exploits coincidence to make what is impossible for black people possible. Coincidence then provides an escape hatch from the myriad difficulties laid out in the plot. Consequently, coincidence in melodrama is powerfully appealing and useful to oppressed groups for arriving at some semblance of justice (Gaines 1993: 57). Unlike both Rohmer and African American filmmaker Oscar Micheaux, Collins turns to a magical/marvelous mode that, in effect, enables her not to rely so heavily on plot to deliver grace and, as it were, a form of justice for the Cruz Brothers. To reprise, the "metalanguage" she uses is a powerful vehicle for conveying the truth at a mythical level removed from plot considerations.

Collins's evocation of the possibilities of the magical in the modern involve the use of color, sound, and cinematography. While there are instances in the film where we are transported to a different space bound by illusionistic rules, the boundaries between the magical and the modern are liminal. The film opens with such an instance when the ghost of Victor's father, Poppa, appears to him. The figure of Poppa folds the magical and the marvelous real, both its extraordinariness, and the acceptance of it as ordinary and at times downright annoying.

The appearance of Poppa marks the turbulence of modernity in this sequence on the "relation between the ordinary and dramatic" (Majumdar 2015: 155). The banal is extraordinary in the film, partly because the prospect of an older european american woman sharing meals and conversation with three Puerto Ricans is almost taboo. The film shows characters with the ability to grasp the world outside of their own community; Collins considered Roth's stories to belong to world literature, and she attributed her interest in them to this universalist strain. Like much world literature, the stories seem to belong to their place but also to other places (Franklin 1981: 31; Ronald Gray in Collins [1982] 2015).

The etiology of magical realism in film when compared with literature is radically different in that in film the hallucinatory quality of the imagery acts to terrorize any representational link, decoupling the eye from the gaze. Using Lacan, Jameson (1986) explains that the technical properties of the image and of the use of color, the pressure to discern different reds or blues on screen, its assault on the perception, obscures the axis of action in the film. He argues that color particularly functions in some prelinguistic realm that impinges on the libidinal apparatus, comparable to dreams where the referents are hard to find. In general, he theorizes that magical realism in film loses the linguistic and narrative anchor that high modernist literature maintains. His observations are a useful departure point for considering magical realism in Collins's film.

The Cruz Brothers and Miss Malloy takes recourse to a literary magical realism, or what Alejo Carpentier in the 1920s called "marvelous realism" (Carpentier 2006). He famously insisted that unlike european surrealist artists who attempted to capture dreams and visions, the Latin American artist only had to look around to apprehend the wonders of the new world. The new world was marvelous because of the coexistence of two temporalities in the same space, as exemplified in the opening of *One Hundred Years of Solitude* in the time of the first human beings in a world freshly created, marveling at the modernity of ice. The entrance of modernity also turns out to be marvelous in its initial impact, if not in the longue durée. *The Cruz Brothers* reveals the incongruity of two worlds in the "encounter" between the brothers and Miss Malloy. The film plays between magical and marvelous realism, drawing out the disparities, but uses the literary narrative to reveal a modern less unitary and more plural.

The use of objects is generally associated with "magical realism," but Collins imposes a narrative overlay, gesturing to the marvelous real. The dominance of objects in visual culture was first recognized by Franz Roh, who called the work of German painters George Grosz and Otto Dix "magic realism" in 1925 to describe the exhibition *Neue Sachlichkeit* or New Realism (Roh 1925). The objects then captivate, specifically in that opening sequence of *Cruz Brothers*, which is explosive. A close-up of the bonnet of a blue shiny car fills the frame, the human beings in the car scarcely visible. No sooner does one of the men get out of the car when a voice over with a dire warning plunges us into the mysterious. Victor responds to the voice's remonstrances as he alights from the car and walks straight into the camera, speaking to a Poppa who is absent in the diegesis. Victor walks towards a car parked in front of him, explaining that he is not stealing the car, merely stripping it, giving us some narrative hint. However, there is a gap in our understanding of where the voice is located and how Victor is listening to it when we cannot locate its source. Poppa's story of the Cortezes and the Cruzes produces a long caesura in the action while Victor starts the car, crashes it, and then runs away with his brothers, with Poppa providing the narrative flourish, "They run away like scared rabbits." The adventure of the brothers is in one time, the voice of Poppa is in the pastness of the past, obtruding in the present, changing the complexion of the "now."

The suggestion that the magical realist surfaces of the objects dispenses with narrative does not hold for this segment of the film. Rather, Collins offers us narrative surplus that transforms the magical real into the kind of mythical realism that Carpentier had envisioned when he detailed the "realism" of Latin America. The scene that follows after the boys run away from the car plumps on the side of narrative, banishing the glittering power of objects and images. In its place, sound dominates, substituting for the object a loud gun-shot, immediately followed by the voice over of Poppa. Poppa has the honor of filling the narrative lacuna left from the first sequence, explaining in matter-of-fact terms that he had been shot and killed in a bank heist gone awry but had triumphed by digging himself out to watch over the boys, as, we might add, ancestors are supposed to. Outside of the narration of the apparatus, we also have a narrator in Poppa, who is named. The density of the narration is unorthodoxly accentuated by the total blackness of the screen as Poppa holds forth. It appears to be a deliberate move not to allow the image pride of place, but to stress the narrative continuity in the diegesis, even if initiated by an extra-diegetic, fleshless voice. Notwithstanding his diegetic absence, Poppa's narrative serves to function as exposition to the diegesis, kindly letting the audience know that only his son can hear him. The voice as trace is remarkably light-hearted, and is oddly inserted into the diegetic time, unlike other magical realist narratives where the story has already been written, as with the Melquíades book in Sanskrit that foretells the story of Macondo's Buendías.

The voice also traverses space and gives us a bridge to the next sequence where Victor has another shiny object, a tape recorder, in his hand. The machine's magical properties exceed their technical function in that it is used for the grand purpose of narration that Poppa claims is a family occupation, quite a translation of the hereditary offices of the West African griot. Yet, the machine is a marker of a particular modernity that is sharply juxtaposed with the objects of art in Miss Malloy's house.

Despite this juxtapositioning, the film does not reprise a recognizable form of third world and more specifically Latin American magic realism. Jameson's definition is relevant for the light it throws on the entrance into modernity, and its debris that the film captures. Turning to the modes of production and their manifestation in form, Jameson concludes:

> The possibility of magic realism as a formal mode is constitutively dependent on a type of historical raw material in which disjunction is structurally present; or to generalize the hypothesis more starkly, magic realism depends on a content which betrays the overlap or the coexistence of precapitalist with nascent capitalist or technological features. (Jameson 1986: 311)

In the context of the film, the ancien régime of high capitalism exists in uneven terms with a rising monopoly capitalism even as the vast majority have no capital. Miss Malloy's house, broken down as it is, figures the decline of a former high capitalism in a town in shambles, where even wages are not an option. The situation is further complicated because race and its historically unequal relationship to capital and the modes of production is not a factor in Jameson's formulation. Thus, the film's modality works within the counterpoints of a perceived, but flawed, sharper disjuncture between the nostalgia for capital and desire for technological features. Capital as such is imbricated only by its absence, and is signaled in culture by apophasis. Consequently, it is through cultural references that the disjuncture is revealed to be a lie, uncovered by the developing friendship between the Cruz brothers and Miss Malloy.

The object itself of course became a work of art during a period of consumer capitalism, where the mode was high modernist, as with Fernand Léger's paintings and his film *Ballet Mécanique* (1924). When the Cruz brothers go to Miss Malloy's house to help restore it, they experience a nostalgia for a time represented by objects that they themselves had not experienced but which had been glamourized by the motion picture industry. The objects here then become detached from their referents, while the objects in the Cruz household retain their use and referential value. The melancholic nostalgia that both groups feel, however, ties the objects even more forcefully into the semiotic chain, almost sharing a past that historically they had not and, more to the point, could not have. Their being together in the present, in the aura of the objects, bridges the abyss between the woman who presumably had experienced those times and the boys who had no ken of them. Where Jameson stresses disjuncture, I would point to coexistence of different spatialities and temporalities that is revealed through a Carpentierian marvelous modernism. All of them, the female throwback to high capitalism, the Puerto Rican boys who will likely never know what capital is, are in this modern moment where technology and object both narrate, where both have a longing for the time that is now and the time that is past. Seemingly separated by the chasm of race and time, their sense of being outside, of time for one, and of capital for another, links them to the universal.

The film presents the fissure between the Cruz brothers and Miss Malloy and, after the development of the friendship, the bridging of the chasm. Walking in single file through the darkness of the early dawn, the brothers come up against Miss Malloy's mansion, brilliantly lit up and quite imposing, mysterious, but inviting, almost in deliberate contrast to the opening tracking in *Citizen Kane* (1941) where the house is forbidding. The low angle shot close to the building, the camera looking up to the roof of the house, catches the flowers in the foreground. A cut takes us to a lotus pond, adding to the sense of a slight (ir)reality. The greens and the blood red of the lotuses in the pond are sharp and incredible, but are not unmoored from references, as Jameson would have it. The pond is a contrast to the derelict street the boys live in, and while the view of both the house and the pond is not sutured to the look of any of the boys, the narrative carries the weight, not of their visual stimulation but of their deeper understanding of this new location. In terms of what Teshome Gabriel has theorized as "nomadic" thought, concepts of the real are not exclusively rooted in empirical seeing. He argues that the real is "both tangible/seeable and untouchable/unseeable. What is not necessarily seeable and touchable, but which nevertheless exists, is merely an extension of known reality" (Gabriel 2001: 396). Note that existence does not depend exclusively on our being able to see and touch it. The Cruz brothers wander into a new reality, incredible because it may be tangible or it may be effervescent. The camera slowly and hesitantly tracks towards Miss Malloy, and equally slowly tracks up to reveal her full figure. A cut to the boys shows them looking at her; they are separated by the pond. Yet, her opening words embrace them warmly: "Welcome, welcome to my house. I am so pleased you could come, boys." The density of the foliage, its lushness, is not in the least paradisiac. As Miss Malloy says, it needs "sprucing up." That it carries tinges of both the magical, or the electrically shocking, and the marvelous (the wonders of the existing) is undeniable, but the overall effect of magical and marvelous realism in the film is created less by the mise-en-scène, a more conventional locus for the magical real, than it is by the proximity of the boys with Miss Malloy. Victor, for instance, insists on following Miss Malloy when she shows them her house, and picks Miss Malloy up when she falls in her dining room. Felix continues to work with his brother although he is more than a little alarmed by Miss Malloy's strange use of words. While the mise-en-scène is not the main factor in the world delineated in the sequence, it adds a dimension to the marvelous

Figure 4.1 *Cruz Brothers*: Miss Malloy greets the brothers

real occurrence of the encounters between the Cruz brothers and Miss Malloy.

The very banal evening tea is turned into an extraordinary occurrence because of the cultural unpreparedness of the audience and of the characters in the diegesis for such an ordinary act across cultures. The sequence opens with a stationary camera showing the boys walking across a green clearing; the camera holds even after the boys have walked away from the clearing, and then shakily moves to show them by the water, on brownish-reddish rocks that the green clearing throws into relief. This simple transition from the house to the outdoors again privileges a narrative sensibility, following the boys' thinking about this new job and the development of their relationship with Miss Malloy. It is only after this crucial narrative glue is provided that there is a cut that shows the boys working and talking, again about this new and unusual situation. An off camera voice announces tea time, and then again, the camera follows Felix rushing up and going to Miss Malloy before Miss Malloy walks into the space as though on to a stage, carrying a silver salver and goblets. That small move of not following up the off camera voice with Miss Malloy provides narrative space, an expansion that differs from uses of magical realism in the novel, notwithstanding the film's appropriation of literary narrative techniques. The novel would feature a rapid movement from one happening to another, linked by ineffable connections, particularly of family; and in film, it would be a surfeit of visual imagery intended to be extreme. Rather, here, the pace is casual, and when the boys come up to get their ginger ale, the utter naturalness of the image takes over. José, enthusiastic as usual, confides in Miss Malloy that her house is like a movie, using exactly the same words he had used for their own rough-and-tumble lodgings. But the two houses could not be more different. José's comment reflects a nostalgia for the movies that conjures up an aura, a glow of contentment in very disparate mise-en-scènes.

Nostalgia films use very specific mise-en-scènes, costumes, and props to produce a different period. *The Cruz Brothers* is very firmly set in the present, but creates glimpses of a hypothetical past, avoiding attempts to construct the "real" of history. The "mood" of nostalgia evoked by the setting and objects in Miss Malloy's house leads to that marvelous real of two coterminous times (Sprengler 2009). As magical realism is very often a function of the surface, so is nostalgia on screen. However, this scene out in the open neither offers a present soaked in itself and denying the past, nor does it act to subvert the present, both possibilities in nostalgia film as theorized by Jameson. Rather, the gaps in understanding among the brothers on the past, and the brothers and Miss Malloy on the present, suggest a modernist mode of looking for both present and past. The nostalgia, tinged with both joy and melancholy, that impels Miss Malloy to retrieve the past through the settings and the surface translates in terms of the marvelous real for the brothers. While Miss Malloy recounts grand events held in the house with a touch of pathos, rooted in loss, José grins widely, concretizing and grasping the historical real submerged by movie nostalgia but apparent in this living character who appears to have stepped out of both the movies and her own past (Jameson 1991).

Until recently, any whiff of nostalgia in film was met with critical suspicion, particularly by Jameson, who argued that these films packaged a past that existed only with references to surfaces and objects. However, Linda Hutcheon among others has pointed out that nostalgia also expresses a route to discerning the past (2003: 94). When José says poignantly, "We don't have any records," he is articulating a desire to have a usable past and, barring that, finding a past, even if it were not his own. Firstly, nostalgia for Miss Malloy's memories affords the space for the marvelous real, but secondly, it also underlines the distance in the present; thus, Collins depicts the present real in complex terms that fold in coterminous temporalities and distinct ruptures.

Miss Malloy's nostalgia acts as the desire of the narrative and, in the Kristevan sense, the desire of the language of the narrative (Kristeva [1969] 1982: 56–7). It is her fancy to restore her place to its former glory, and when she ropes the boys in, they become part and parcel of her nostalgia film but one with obtrusions that jostle the narrative line of nostalgia. She says, for instance, as she is recounting tales of parties in the house, that her husband was quite brutish during the day but acceptable in the evenings. She does not rush headlong into memories but says aloud, "Step gently into the past." Her nostalgia is further complicated by a feeling of having mislaid the past, while wishing to reclaim it: "I am looking for my life. Will you help me look for it?" She says in a trance-like state to Victor that, "It is somewhere in the house." And earlier, she had asked José if he felt drawn to the house. The house as a symbol of the anterior past being dragged into the past in the present convolutes any simple narrative line on nostalgia. A countervailing narrative thread threatens to ignore the impetus behind the restoration. Felipe systematically breaks the narrative flow when the nostalgic intersects with the marvelous, usually by loud bangings and clatterings that brings the action to a halt. And then there is Victor, who seems to be supremely blitheful, merely seeing Miss Malloy as a slightly crazy person and the job as just a job. He repeats this twice to Felipe, easily accepting this relationship on those terms, but inevitably identifying the nostalgia house project as the only basis of their relationship with Miss Malloy. It is José who is most drawn into Miss Malloy's world, at first in jest, miming the movies, but later with some earnestness that adds richness and density to both their characters. They start practicing romantic lines with each other and dancing, but the game is too dangerous for José, who finally cries out that they talk differently and that they think differently.

The scenes that are marked by nostalgia are not in every instance meant to evoke pathos. When José first sees the house, it does, but the conduit is the cinema. A later scene dwells on this motif by setting the action up to reconstitute a nostalgia movie scene. Dressed in period clothes, the brothers come wearing contrasting, old-fashioned suits: Victor in white and José in black. Miss Malloy is dressed in a white, flowing dress recalling not just the 1950s but perhaps garden parties of an even earlier era, largely already imagined through the movies. Stumbling upon this scene during the middle of his jobbing day, Felipe is shocked and seems to have lost his bearings. Collins sets up a movie scene that has a spectator who absorbs the surface as the real, riveted by the exterior. The scene's structural integrity in the diegesis is shattered when Felipe hoarsely calls a halt to the music and to the action of the scene being enacted. He appeals to a higher authority in calling for Poppa. The magical real is shattered even as all of them seem suspended between the real and the magical real for an instant.

The mise-en-cadre of the dance sequence in the ground clearing is the stage for the limits of the association between the brothers and Miss Malloy. However, even as some of the codes of the nostalgia film—the style of movement, the actors in a world of their own—are used, Felipe's interruption places the moment in the present, bringing us back to the idea that the surface of the magical real insists on the presentness of the modern, thus counterbalancing the pastness of nostalgia films. The modes of

Figure 4.2 *Cruz Brothers*: Nostalgia or desire?

the magical real put pressure on the trope of nostalgia to make use of it for the present. Poppa's coda underlines these seemingly unruly crossings across time and space: "The spell is broken," and crucially, their wallets are "fat." But when he insists that his sons are legends, Victor, framed by the same window-space featured in the opening of the film, snaps that this is not true, and that it had taken a bank robbery and a death to get them here; that there is nothing large about the Cruz brothers at all. The film systematically cycles back to the opening, the epic mythical structure belying Victor's words. The brothers are left with a car as a legacy and their wages. The last sequence of their traipsing across the park, with the same soundtrack accompaniment, leaves us in no doubt, at least, of the existence of the marvelous real in the concrete trace of their friendship with Miss Malloy.

The counterpoise maintained by the magical real and the marvelous real renders the narrative of the *Cruz Brothers* modernist in modality and in narrative. Thus, Jameson's contention that the film medium cannot anchor the narrative in the magical real modality is not accurate as a generalization. The film's modernist narration is contrived by use of tactics prevalent during the silent film era.[2]

A brief look at the history of borrowings across the arts of film and literature throws partial light on the "translation" of language that Collins sought. In *Cruz Brothers*, Collins avails of qualities in film that were prominent during the silent era, patterns that impressed themselves on modernist form, particularly with respect to the interiority she is able to narrate in the film. A strain of film criticism now holds that the modernist narrative in fiction would not have been possible without its germination in film, specifically because modernist techniques across the arts trumped all differences, while highlighting the extended possibilities of each medium. Eisenstein (1949), for instance, writes of how enthralled Joyce was to know of innovations Eisenstein was making in projecting interiority and the interior monologue. Apparently Joyce, although almost blind, insisted on watching these pieces, showing how influential formal experiments across modernist literature and film are. Eisenstein recalls: "When Joyce and I met in Paris, he was intensely interested in my plans for the inner film-monologue, with a far broader scope than is afforded by literature" (1949: 104). Further silent film through its use of intertitles without speech showed how silence could be used effectively in modernist narration, particularly to heighten one of its richest elements, ambiguity, and with it the possibility of change, or the open-ending. The silences in *Cruz Brothers* are caesuras that invite reflection on the conflict between a universalism that strains against the realist and an ethnicity spawned by exclusion: the standpoint of the two Cruz brothers and Miss Malloy on the one hand, and Felipe on the other.

The dance scene in the clearing that is at once a nostalgia clip for the audience and a frightening reality for the spectator, Felipe, takes advantage of the rich philosophical possibilities engendered by silence, accentuated by the serene, gracious silence in the diegetic dance sequence. The soundtrack playing during the dance sequence is of a piece with nostalgia filmic codes, slow and based on Romantic music from the western classical music tradition. As in silent films, the music functions as more than a mood piece and carries narrative weight in suggesting harmony, grace, design. When Felipe comes out of hiding and stares at them, the two Cruz brothers and Miss Malloy are silent and the narrative itself is held suspended in its dream-like state. The marvelous appears to cross over from the dancers on the green to the reluctant voyeur who hears the music, even though it has no diegetic source. And when he screams, "Stop the music," we are met with a wholly different silence that envelops them all. A punctum, the silence hints at thoughts and desires articulated in the only language available.

The cinematography in this penultimate dance sequence is shot with a view to creating an aura of the enchanted. Medium shots place, firstly, Miss Malloy in the clearing ground, secondly, Victor, and then José. One close-up threatens the fragility of the magic when José crushes Miss Malloy to him, dragging in the here and now, once again almost, but not quite, interlacing two temporalities. Although Collins has to use cuts to show us José approaching the clearing ground, she relies on pans almost exclusively during the dance and includes all the characters in the shot when José intervenes. The magical realist–marvelous realist mode is enhanced by this cinematographic style that does not follow the shot/reverse shot paradigm, followed by cuts, to feed the narrative vehicle. Consequently, although the magical–marvelous realist mode seems incompatible with the essai film's traditional adherence to conversation to further ideas, the film avoids the "what happens next" model to pause on how the characters' emotional sensibilities are being developed. In lieu of reacting to the possibility of change through action, or dialogue, the film uses realism and the magical marvelous to push its audience gently out of the specificity of its own time and location.

Notes

1 Myth for Collins was to be differentiated from the "mythologizing" of black characters as sinners or saints, that is, as outsiders who are hollowed-out projections of the white psyche (Franklin 1980; Collins [1984a] 2015).
2 As a teacher of film, Collins used silent film extensively, and the eight short films her students were asked to make had to be silent and highlight one particular formal element in the making of film, an exercise that made her intensely aware of how to use silence to narrate (Collins 1984a).

5

Sacred doubles

Collins's use of magical realism in the 1980s is all the more incongruent, given that it was the heyday of the "New Realism" in African American film, defined by time, specifically black people's time, and urban mise-en-scènes. The films in the realist-temporal paradigm—*Boyz N the Hood, Juice, Straight Out of Brooklyn, Deep Cover*—as distinct from the expressive-spatial, revolve around young boys becoming men (Diawara 1993: 23). That Collins should have chosen another route to initiate three Puerto Rican boys into a semblance of adulthood is perhaps more comprehensible when one regards magical–marvelous realism as a mode that provided her with a narrative solution, one that sorted out the story and, equally importantly, followed a universalist principle in the rudimentary forms that were expressed or stifled by the characters in *Cruz Brothers*. An "expressive" film, it touches upon the male's rite of passage into adulthood that the later "new realist" films would. Collins's transformation of the coming-of-age story was released in the early part of the decade when filmic imaginings of the Puerto Rican community and the Latinx community were predictably both vulgar and broad, continuing a pattern established in the early part of the twentieth century (Lopez 1991; Woll 1981). *Cruz Brothers* is prescient about staging conversations in sharp contrast to the black–white, Latino/a–white relationships in the realist, time-oriented films along the lines of Melvin Van Peebles's *Sweet Sweetback's Baadasssss Song* (1971) that "recognizes nationalist narratives as enabling strategies for survival, empowerment, and self-determination" (Diawara 1993: 9).

Losing Ground, like *Cruz Brothers*, sidesteps the nationalist narrative, is even less invested in the national allegory, and identifies the human as the core of storytelling: the story emerges from the individual's place in the community, and the community's response to the nation's interpellation of marginal subjects. Even as the national is incorporated, its imaginary does not inform the narrative nucleus. Discussing the craft of filmmaking, Collins maintained that storytelling involves using language to sort out the narrative tangles human beings create. In other words, she does not allegorize race; rather, she pays attention to black subjects and their difficulties in the community and in the nation. The solutions she veers towards have universal applicability, an anomaly, in general, in the US since the 1960s, when one version or another of identity politics, not to detract at all from its progressive goals and results, has dominated. It is important to reiterate that the predicaments the characters find themselves in arise from the ideas the characters have, rather than in the action or, as would seem expected for a drama, in conflict (Nicholson 1988/9: 12).

Losing Ground locates the dilemma of the text in the characters of Sara Rogers, a philosophy professor, and her husband Victor, an artist. The film's abstract plot pursues the relationship between questions of identity and philosophies of art. While this theme is developed in terms of the debate about the value of art and of philosophy, and the role of passion in both, there are other structural elements in the film that add a particular gendered dimension to the essai film—indeed, a feminist one—by importing Romance genre elements from literature and, oddly, romcom elements from mainstream film, here mixed with African American traditions that reveal the limitations of each genre for the exploration of an intellectual black woman's personal and professional life.

The dimensions of the essai film are expanded in that the existential speculations that Sara entertains of her identity are complicated by her internalizing her husband's views on the insufficiency of her discipline, philosophy, which according to Victor inhibits her from accessing the complex fullness of the abstract and the sensory that he experiences. The film follows Sara's quest to discover the richness of the philosophical in mysticism. Her research follows this path, an untypical way of attempting to fulfill a quest. Moreover, this quest is entangled in the mundane of everyday married life: a commonplace interest in communicating with her husband who seems lost in a world of his own, and even less aware of her own needs, but drags her into his, dismissing her objections. That Collins intertwines these themes is significant mainly because African American films had only infrequently ventured to explore personal/romantic and intellectual relationships, in part because of the film industry's inability to conceive of black lives outside the racial imaginary. However, exploring inter-personal relationships, particularly in a romantic vein, is crucial to establish African Americans as human beings first, who participate in the simple and simultaneously grand universal journey of love and its many anguishes. When asked what *Losing Ground* was about, Collins is reported to have said, "a young woman falling in love and making a mess of it" (Hachard 2015). Two generic strands intersect in this film—essai and Romance—within an African diaspora framework.

The essai

Discussion of personal problems is ubiquitous in the essai film, particularly conversations about relationships, starting with Godard's *Breathless* (1960) where the two main characters lie in bed and talk about how many lovers they have had in the past in conjunction with what books they have read. Truffaut's *Jules and Jim* (1962) is an extended elaboration of the development of relationships, largely predicated on character. And of course, the Rohmer films that Collins admired are replete with long philosophical conversations that include soul searching about relationships. The human drama in these films invariably revolves around some version of a romantic connection. This is certainly true of *Losing Ground*; however, there are very few conversations about relationships except obliquely through disagreements about art and philosophy. The viewer begins to grasp that these intellectual divergences also reveal Victor's imperviousness to Sara's world view, what Sara later clarifies as the "unequal" nature of their relationship. Sara has a warm relationship with her mother, to whom she talks openly about Victor's routine infidelity. The conversation between mother and daughter introduces the theme of black women's community, a motif that is central to all Sara's writings. As Sara confides in her mother, their emotional and intellectual sustenance of each other as black women and black women artists becomes apparent. Sara spends less time talking about the object of her affections, Victor, than she does about her own work. She conveys the exuberance she feels when she knows intuitively that she has arrived at the heart of the matter:

> The actual sex doesn't bother me ... The only thing I've ever known like that [trance-like state] is sometimes in the middle of writing a paper my mind suddenly takes this *tremendous* leap into a new interpretation of the material ... I *know* I'm right. I *know* I can prove it ... my head starts dancing like crazy ... (Collins 1991: 165)

Sara adds that she feels somehow despondent that the exultation is based on *thinking* and longs for that trance-like state for herself outside the strict purview of paper writing. Her response is in part informed by Victor's unthinking reflection of the western metaphysical binaries separating the intellect from emotion; yet, her engagement with the issue is feminist in that she questions these rigid oppositions that inevitably carry racial and gender assignations. She is in search of a history of philosophy that would enable her to comprehend both without sacrificing her training or succumbing to some western construction of black people as instinctual without the ability to think rationally. The issue is specific for Sara's gender and ethnicity; it would not be so for the male intellectual in the western tradition, as seen in Rohmer's *My Night with Maud*.

While Rohmer follows the principle of not drawing attention to the film form lest it detract from the narrative and the discussion, Collins takes a different tack, bringing in the verve of the dramatist in this conversation between Sara and her mother, an actor. *My Night with Maud* uses long takes to imitate the literary, and "subtle blocking" of the conversation between the three characters to underplay the cinematic in the sequence (Holland n.d.). Like Rohmer, Collins also avoids the repetitive shot/reverse shots that are routine in the Hollywood master/tutor code, and gently dollies from Sara to her mother during the conversation. The tone of the conversation could not be further from the debate in *My Night with Maud*. Sara and her mother are laughing, chatting, and discussing issues in an everyday way, thinking about themselves through ideas that are relatively new to them, but throughout saturated by their emotional sense of what the trance-like state might mean for each of them. They are passionate about it, and there is considerable warmth in the exchange, modeling the development of ideas through empathy and affirmation rather than argumentation. They are not, so to speak, human beings who are vessels for abstract ideas which Rohmer's characters, barring slight disturbances, appear to be, their actions fueling further thinking on moral issues. The protagonist of *My Night with Maud* is not given a name, suggesting his allegorical role. Sara and her mother are flesh-and-blood creatures. When Sara describes her own transports, she moves her head forward, miming the dancing she feels her head undergoes when she is out of herself. Both leave the morality out of it entirely, her mother commenting that she does not know if it is the gods that "have" her or Satan.

The visual palette is startling different from Rohmer's; Collins uses color and the mise-en-scène to suffuse the scene with a sense of warmth and life. Medium shots show the proximity of the two conversationalists and their intimacy. The notion of the essai film in this context is expanded to seek out new philosophical positions that the women are in the process of discovering, not securing moral positions that have already been defined as in Rohmer. *Losing Ground* also distinguishes itself from the philosophizing in Godard's *Breathless*, and from the social philosophy in Truffaut's *Jules and Jim*, foregrounding race in the intricate connection between the philosophical idea and the gendered, raced self.

Romance

The Romance genre, and its offshoot in the American novel, are hostile to African American subject material. The sentimental novel of the nineteenth century followed a virtuous female, who during the course of the novel establishes her value to the male and is rewarded by his appreciation of her. The sentimental novel then always concluded with the marriage of the female hero to the object of her affections. For African American women writers in the nineteenth century, the plot was out of bounds, given that the definition of a virtuous woman was solely the property of euro-american women; the sexual assault and rape of black women consigned them to a class outside the virtuous, and even outside womanhood (Carby 1987). Consequently, novelists took recourse to the black woman's "uplift" work to prove her virtue and womanhood. This trope is picked up then by African American film, including Oscar Micheaux's oeuvre *Within Our Gates* (1919) and *Body and Soul* (1925), which feature black female protagonists pursued by men, black and white. The female's affiliation to the progress of her race finally redeems her, and in some cases culminates in marriage. Thus, given the weight of history against the female hero's quest being completely fulfilled, Collins opts against a utopian ending, giving us instead a modernist one, replete with ambiguity. This is compounded by the fact that the romcom dilemma of the communication channels between husband and wife also remains unresolved. The careful detailing of the difficulties in the husband and wife's romantic relationship is of moment precisely because it normalizes and humanizes black subjects in that most powerful of all arenas—the romantic.

The trance-like experience as a quest motif is mystical, in not translating either into a treasure or a romantic object. Nevertheless, it does serve as the desire of the narrative. As the philosopher protagonist becomes more aware of her data's overwhelmingly western framework, she is frustrated in her need to be transported to another state of mind. Underlining the importance of the experience of black women, it is Sara's mother who brings up the possibilities offered by non-western philosophies, touching on a key concept in Haitian philosophy, possession. Sara turns to Haitian philosophy, specifically Louis Mars's work on possession in vaudun.[1] The philosopher Louis Mars connects the emotional with the intellectual, noting that possession fills the subject with "the consciousness of an immediate rapport with desire" ([1946] 1977: 11). Moreover, the rite is deeply spiritual in that none other than the gods arrive in the service of the humans.

Developing her ideas on a philosophy that emerges from Africa, in counterpoint to the time in the opening sequence devoted to western philosophers, Collins features yet another scene of Sara engrossed in the intellectual endeavor. The sequence of Sara in the library recalls the trope of literacy in African American literature; the material presence of books and paper suggests that for Sara, the intellectual, these instruments perform the same function that canvas and brush do for her artist husband Victor. A slow tracking shot catches the medieval statuary of monks, all a uniform rust-like color, before it lights upon Sara, her back to the camera, head bent over the typewriter, a sign of her engagement in creative activity. Halfway through, we hear Sara's voice off screen, carrying the authority of the voice over.' We listen to what she is typing, and even as she talks about the gods mounting the individual, the individual being possessed, the camera dollies upward to show a frieze. The art appears to be all european, familiar objects signifying "europe" in almost any context; yet the european backdrop here is a piquant reminder, both of the absence of the non-european in philosophy, and Professor Rogers's contribution to expanding that canon. After enumerating the stages of possession, Sara concludes her thesis saying that "the ecstasy is after the fact."

Louis Mars's treatise on ecstasy through possession functions as a sub-text and introduces the informing myth, the vaudun ritual that culminates in the dance between Sara and Duke in the metafilm. It is important to see how else vaudun performance rites make an entrance into the film. According to vaudun myth, the gods possess those who have pleased them, and further, it is through dance that humans experience their presence: "In kinetic-emotive mysticism, a god reveals himself to man through the brutal breaking up of self" (Mars [1946] 1977: 15). The performative aspect of vaudun draws out the ecstasy of the dancer in the film within the film. Possessed by the gods/the ancestors, the dancer loses herself in the other.

The dance itself is charged with meaning and operates on both the syntagmatic level and the associative or the Barthesian paradigmatic level (Barthes 1994). The ultimate dance that Sara has with Duke in the film within the film is to be distinguished from the previous dance she had with him during rehearsal, where the sequence shot against the background of a New York building largely appears to be what it is: a take for a movie. And when her "rival" comes, the whole is tepid and plebeian. Sara and Duke are chatting through this dance and the sequence itself is amusing and entertaining, giving no indication of the significance of the theme of the dance in the plot of the film. The last dance, however, is completely explosive in contrast, and when Duke (Johnny) starts dancing with the other girl, with the same sinuous moves, Sara (Frankie) blasts him away. The dance infers that Sara, "possessed" by Frankie, herself possessed by a spirit, shoots and kills her lover.

At the associative or paradigmatic level, entire systems of signification are condensed in the dance. The dance transports Sara into a trance akin to the experience of being possessed, challenging the western notions of the self that suffuse Victor's thinking. Victor's version of the trance-like state celebrates the experience of the self, unlike the vaudun ritual that involves the self being inhabited by another. For Sara, the trance involves both the self and the other.

In the diegesis, Victor has disparaged Sara for her dancing skills. Yet, here her dance is of a higher order, not comparable to Victor's flirtatious dance steps as prelude to sex. Sara's dancing with Duke yields fresh insights about her character not just to Victor, the viewer on screen, but also to the viewers off screen. The passion inherent in the movements, particularly when Sara kicks her leg high, is a startling revelation of the wellsprings of the erotic in her. The directions for the dance, based on the African American ballad, add another layer of density to the performance, recalling a perennial trope of the betrayal of the black woman. The very inclusion of the musical in the folkloric roots *Losing Ground* in the African American oral/performative tradition, regarded as the "positive" site of instruction in comparison with the negative moorings of the visual.

From a received feminist perspective, the spectacle of the dance, of the female performer, would seem to reify her as the old archetype of the female entertainer, the Jezebel, or in high culture terms, the tragic mulatta. However, other feminist theorists have argued that when the male viewer in the diegesis is denied visual pleasure, as Victor is in this instance, the male gaze trajectory is less than relevant (Ramanathan 2006). Further, in terms of the syntagma of the narrative, the specularization of the black woman is irrelevant; indeed, it is her visibility that is at stake. In the dance, Sara, and other black women conjured up by her presence, is "seen."

The structure of the film, and the use of the film within the film at the conclusion, is modernist in not committing itself to classical closure, and feminist in signaling that the resolution has served the female hero. The historical adds weight to the philosophical dimension of the vaudun rite. Where the vaudun ritual celebrates the gods' possession of the individual, here it is an ancestral figure from a representation, rooted in the language and idioms of the people, that possesses her. The intensity of the dance summons Frankie, as it were, who blows Johnny away.

During the course of her scholarly exploration of ecstasy, Sara Rogers seeks answers from a psychic. Coming right after Sara's intense study of vaudun in the library when it seems that she has her thesis hammered out, the sequence of her visit to the psychic taps into Sara's vague uneasiness about the future and a level of insecurity about the conclusion of her research. Offered as a narrative possibility, the sequence links the psychic with the personal as Sara asks the psychic to read her metaphysical makeup. In place of the deus ex machina of Greek tragedy, or the marvelous realism of *The Cruz Brothers*, minor characters fulfill a function in the plot that bridges the unforeseeable and the everyday. To some extent they are what one critic calls "agents of narrative resolution to the Greek concept of *moira*" (Bruce Robbins qtd in Kurnick 2011: 89). The sequence links Sara's increasingly urgent existential questions to the last scene of the film where, as Frankie, she shoots Johnny. She walks into the female psychic's arbor, an outdoor space in contrast to the many interiors, indicating the exploratory nature of the visit. There she asks the psychic directly what she, the psychic, feels "inside" herself when she sees a person. The question returns to the notion of doubleness raised by the reading of Louis Mars but gets absolutely no response from the psychic, who says she does not understand. Sara then shifts to a different theme that is more personal, yet framed by the impersonal. Can the psychic read her future? The psychic gives her a rendition of her meeting a tall, dark stranger with a top hat and being photographed with him. This reference to the film within the film where Sara would be paired with Duke is a seeming throwaway but does seem to prophesy a particular "destiny" for Sara. As a character, this is the psychic's only appearance. She has no interaction with any of the other characters and, in that sense, does not enter the "character-system" of the film, and barely takes up narrative space, in part because the space is located outside of the characters in the diegesis, thus adding to her what I call extra-narrative function, as revealer rather than motivator of action (Woloch 2003: 13). However, unlike Brechtian epic drama where the audience knows what will happen, here the scene is used to connect the realistic mode of the film with the Romance aspect, only to be muddied again by the inconclusive final scene with its overladen apparatus. The scene with the psychic ends in the most noncommittal way. Sara walks away, back to her apartment and Victor; it would appear that nothing at all had happened.

The psychic is not the only minor character whose role is easy to overlook in the film. Several other minor characters, complicated by the motif of doubling as a discursive strategy, enlarge the film's philosophical thinking on black women. The modernist doppelgänger trope, two characters in the story who are alter egos, is amplified by extending the trope to include multiple asymmetrical versions of doubling.

Soon after the protagonist Sara and her husband Victor come to their summer place in upstate New York, Victor paints Sara in their apartment. She is seated in an embrasure in the window, her profile partly lighted, accentuating the atelier atmosphere of the apartment. The scene purposefully imports the values of painting and, in its stillness, resembles one. Victor also paints Celia, a Puerto Rican woman he meets in the town. At the diegetic level, the two women appear to be foils, rather than doppelgängers, because of the difference in their personalities. However, the fact that Victor is painting Celia equates Celia and Sara at the structural level, both models for the male artist. That the two women serve as subject material for the male artist is not the only indication of doubling between them. The second instance is more complex, as it involves the film within the film and brings us into the terrain of versions or covers of women. Celia is glimpsed dancing by the water on her own, again out in the open, and shot using cinematic techniques. When Sara later, in the film within the film, dances, we are met with an almost uncanny doubling: of Celia and Sara, and of Sara and Frankie.

The doubles in the film are not exact replicas or "covers." The traditional double is simultaneously subject and somebody other, someone who stalks the subject like death. The characters in *Losing Ground* are tangential doubles, so that when Sara "becomes" Frankie, the question is not whether Sara dies but

Figure 5.1 *Losing Ground*: Sara and Duke in the metafilm

whether she has come to life, following the ancient rite of vaudun where the subject is inhabited by the gods. The double questions the original characterization of the subject and casts representation into a crisis. The doubling does not arise naturally, or from the diegesis, as in traditional doppelgänger films such as *Dr. Jekyll and Mr. Hyde* (dir. Mamoulian, 1931) and thus is anti-mimetic, lifting the character out of the diegesis and provoking philosophical questions outside of identity, and of the provisionality and threat of being itself (Mellier 2018).

The "doubling" that Sara enacts, or experiences, pushes us into the realm of the unconscious, the cinema its metonym. One is tempted to theorize the postmodern here because of the proliferation of images; however, replicas do not carry their own identities. Celia and Sara do. Thus, the doppelgänger motif is within the purview of that modernist theme of "the secret sharer": Celia and Sara's presence as minority women. Where Sara's doubling as Frankie is featured within the extra-diegetic, Frankie, as the literary source, escapes both the diegetic and the extra-diegetic, the uncanny ghost in the diegetic, whose very existence in the historical and social is transmuted by her story and spirit being channeled here. Even as a minor character, Frankie's role is multivalent; she represents the betrayed black woman in the folk ballad in all its rich socially concrete dimension. She also invokes moira, or destiny for colored women, brought into the mix by Celia, serving as a double for Sara. The doubling is further densely layered when we consider yet another colored female minor character, the female who plays the role of Frankie's rival. Within this design, as a double she plays the "other woman." The asymmetry of the doubling here is critical for it helps us understand that the rival is a double of Celia, but since Celia herself is a double of Sara, the distinctions between the women fall apart. In the penultimate sequence that Frankie and Johnny dance, Johnny firmly drags Frankie to the side and makes his way to her "rival," but the ease with which he does it shows that this dancer too will be cast aside. The asymmetry of the doubling links

Figure 5.2 *Losing Ground*: Johnny betrays Frankie

the women, including Sara's mother, and sets them on the other side of any romantic interchange.

The asymmetrical doubling of the men is striking in pointing to the allegorical role of an important minor character, Duke. Collins had prepared the audience for this role in the manner in which she presents Duke when Sara first encounters him in the library. Duke literally appears out of nowhere, talks philosophy fluently, mentions psychics when telling Sara who he is:

> In this life I'm an out-of-work actor, who once studied for the ministry, in other lives.. so the psychics tell me, I've been an Italian count, an English Lord, even a Confederate soldier. Apparently this is my first incarnation as a Negro ... (Collins 1991: 141–2)

His introduction openly brings in the otherworldly, and his stature, as he stands over Sara working in subdued lighting in the library, is a deliberate nod to a mysterious character, with subtle intimations of a sinister cast. His clothes too are so much a contrast to the clothes of the other men in the film that one is uneasily aware that he may not be entirely substantial in the mortal world. Diegetically, this suspicion is allayed by his being the uncle of Sara's student; nevertheless, visually the image remains paramount. Thus, his allegorical role is resealed in the final dance with Sara. Given that the psychic had predicted the appearance of the tall dark stranger, and it is when Sara dances with Duke that she feels the impact of Frankie's passion, Duke too is in the guise of a Fate, spelling destiny.

The minor characters function as intersectional points that bring the essai and Romance in dialogue. However, it appears a failed venture, as is the more substantial research into the mystical visionary tradition. Yet, the female hero has reached the end of her quest, which, while successful in the extra-diegetic sequence of the dance in metafilm, is unaddressed except through the dance in the metafilm. This narrative solution is one in keeping both with the character and her creative search, and the constraints placed on African American women by the genre of Romance.

In the context of the sustained development of the plot around the artist/philosopher couple's difficulties, it is noteworthy that Victor's characterization does not follow any of the fetishized figurations of black masculinity, or even what Mark Reid dubs the "negritude" version which essentializes black masculinity (Doy 2000; Reid 1997). Victor is allowed to be a human being, not a caricature. Very often, the charge laid against women filmmakers is that the male characters are utterly unrealistic. To some extent, this is true of films that privilege the point of view of women; for example, Dulac's *The Smiling Madame Beudet* and Marleen Gorris's *A Question of Silence* (1982). The criticism itself is blind to how so-called "realistic" representations of women in film merely use the codes of realism to depict women; quite different from presenting them outside male lenses. For the black woman filmmaker, such point of view, personalized, intimate depictions of a husband or male lover are not viable, for they could shore up derogatory stereotypes of black men. Not only would that end be undesirable, but it would also certainly detract from the personal romantic dilemma that is one of the topics of the film.

A key feature of the modern romcom as seen in the Nancy Meyers films are the glossy interiors, the highly polished surfaces, the kitchen spaces that women are in, a reflection of their talent and their affluence. The interior mise-en-scènes that envelop the world of the female hero in the Meyers corpus place her in a space that she is comfortable in, even as it has aspects that suggest that it is a staged setting for her own persona. Interior mise-en-scènes have always been an issue for women in African American film, given that their fixed location was usually in the kitchen. Yet, Collins chooses to make *Losing Ground* almost exclusively in interiors. Elizabeth Alexander explains that the interior functions very differently for black women: the interior is a place where the aesthetics of the woman can be expressed. Therefore, the space is one where the self is made "visible," the living room particularly functioning as a "theatrical space, and, in a still visual realm, a space for tableau or *retablo*, with its connotations of the sacred" (Alexander 2004: 9). Alexander suggests that this kind of presentation is at the core of what curator Valerie Cassel calls Black Romanticism. In the catalogue for the Harlem Museum's exhibition "Black Romantic," Cassel (2002) argues that "Black Romanticism should not be dismissed as fictionalised nostalgia" particularly because it "engages aspects of a vernacularism reservoir." In the film, the interiors are expressive of the male artist rather than the female philosopher. While expressive, the interiors are not Romantic. Given the mise-en-scènes of most Hollywood films featuring African American spaces, the decorative interiors of the two black New York artists would appear fictionalized to audiences of the 1980s.

Contrary to the expectations of the romcom genre that uses aesthetic interiors to frame the female hero, and as noted earlier, Sara's presence—her visibility—is less than apparent when she is posing for Victor, seated in a window embrasure in one corner of the room. Sara is freer when she is dancing with Duke in a huge open-air space. Insofar as interiors are concerned, Collins does not set much stock by domestic interiors within this specific Romantic orientation, but is invested in black women occupying public institutional spaces, such as the library. Most film critics would concede that opening sequences both frame the themes of a film and introduce the main lines of inquiry, or as Annette Insdorf argues, they highlight the "thematic concerns and stylistic approach ... that will be developed throughout subsequent scenes" (2017: preface). *Losing Ground* opens with Sara lecturing to her students, in command of the space. Thus, the film to some extent folds the anti-romcom genre into the essai film.

The perils of romance are severely underlined by Victor's casual, perhaps unthinking, questioning of the creative importance of Sara's philosophical writing, and then further, in the equally casual entitled way Victor humiliates Sara in front of their guests. Rather, intellectual companionship—the friendship between Sara and Duke, and Sara and the student George—is valued. As a minor character, George is perhaps what narratologists might call "flat"; his purpose is purely instrumental in setting up the vaudeville "silent comedy" (Woloch 2003). But as discussed in

Chapter 2, the fact that he, because of being the film's director, is also the surrogate auteur is important in bringing us back from the fate-ridden Romantic tale to the overall modernist exit of the film.

The scene itself is marked as extra-diegetic by the director's instructions, and the illusion of the cinematic rent by an abrupt cut, showing Victor's car. Even as Frankie and his partner dance, George, the director, interrupts with suggestions for precise moves. A cut-in brings Sara into the scene, watching the couple dance. George gives her the final cue. A close-up of Sara's face shows her fear, uncertainty, and anguish. She shoots. Victor reels at the impact. We cut back to Sara, and then to Victor. Both experience some recognition. Sara, we are clear, has experienced ecstasy. The question of "what happens next" remains unanswered. Rather, the modernist narrative solution creates space for new philosophies for African American women; hence, none of the generic strands of the film, including the philosophical, finds full closure.

Note

1   Collins had translated Louis Mars from the French to the English.

6

Film across drama and art

If Collins had been successful in integrating the other performing arts in her films, it was in part due to her extensive experience in drama and her literary efforts, including fiction and screenplays. Her formal instruction in film and her teaching of the craft of filmmaking further enabled her to manipulate each of the arts to enrich the other; to translate stagecraft to filmic properties, to transpose filmic values to her writing. Her interest in the relationship between art and film goes back to her doctoral work in the Sorbonne where her thesis was looking at the conceptual effects of borrowings across the arts with reference to André Breton and "the cinematic notion behind surrealism as they practised it" (Klotman [1982] 2015). Critics have only very recently identified the integration of the arts in her films (O'Malley 2019).

Scholars of silent cinema/primitive cinema have argued that the practitioners of the newest art, whether a Griffith or a Murnau, were engaged in an unconscious internecine warfare with the other representational arts, particularly theatre/literature and painting, film's ancestors. This "rivalry" was very often interwoven into the themes of silent films and the rivalry "settled" in the diegesis itself. Wanting to legitimize itself as a serious art, not just a bastard descendent of vaudeville, film turned to literature, particularly efforts to formalize the narrative apparatus, to achieve literary status. If these early films, such as Griffith's *Broken Blossoms* (1919) and Robert Wiene's *The Cabinet of Dr. Caligari* (1920), exhibited this tension between the arts,

Collins's films reveal the unifying powers of the arts. Even among the New York Black Independents, several of whom embed at least one other art, very often photography, Collins is distinctive in using painting, theatre and literature, and film in both her films. Thus, the films carry the aesthetic values of all three media, even as they fulfill their narrative and philosophical functions.

The film's borrowings from painting have not gone unnoticed by critics: "Post-modern and anti-realist, the film has the look and feel of a painting" (Williams 1994: 38). The deliberate pictorial quality of the film could be viewed as "postmodern" in its self-reflexivity about art and in the caesuras to narrative progress; however, the film is not anti-realist in terms of the definition it sets up for what constitutes realism for black artists. Given the deficit paradigm of African American art in art history, and the paucity of "art" in mainstream film dealing with African Americans, *Losing Ground* purposefully brings the richness of diverse artistic modes together, suggesting possibilities for other African American "art" films (Thompson 2000).

The abstract conflict in *Losing Ground* is between philosophy and art. When the film opens, however, their complementarity is established using the materials of philosophy and of art. In both cases, the materials also evoke a key physical element in the delivery of film—the screen. Sara stands with her face half turned to the blackboard, one arm extended to point to something she has written, the words on the board/screen. A double role is presented here directly: the viewer outside the screen and the viewer who, like the famous Woody Allen character in *The Purple Rose of Cairo* (1985), steps into the screen. The viewer/student gets a lesson on existentialism.

The professor's detached knowledge of the discipline is combined with the human subject's passionate involvement with "thought" and "absurdity." The topics of discussion—the depths of "being" in Sartre, the absurd in Camus—glide by imperceptibly to be developed by the professor's dialogue with students on the motif of the outsider. Of the three French writers mentioned, all are philosophers and also major writers of the twentieth-century

Figure 6.1 *Losing Ground*: The second screen

modernist literary canon. Genet merits the greatest discussion, Sartre some, and Camus is mentioned only once. Nevertheless, the intertextual reference to Meursault, the stranger, is provocative in drawing to our mind the story of a pied-noir in Algeria, neither an Arab nor completely a colonial Frenchman, locating the text in the interstices of a duality that is discomfiting even when the protagonist is part of the colonial establishment. Buried in the layers of the modernist narrative is the story of the native outsider, the Arab, native to Algeria but a foreigner in his own land, shot for no reason other than being in the land. The discursive allusion to the invisible native makes connections across a spectrum to enable scrutiny of colonialism. That Sara speaks so passionately about the plight of the outsider and his/her universal qualities shows the easy flow to and from philosophy and literature in the film's opening exposition and statement.

The next major sequence almost schematically introduces the second term, art, in the abstract conflict between philosophy and art. A medium shot shows a camera slowly taking in the walls with ferns on the table, colorful fabrics, a red sofa, a profusion of colors topped by a small painting, and then at the dead center of the room a huge painting that takes over the whole wall. The functional and ornamental items in the artist's studio seem to be part of a canvas, but an animated one, as the camera is mobile. Unlike Julie Taymor's film on Frida Kahlo, *Frida* (2002), where stillness dominates many of the set-ups to mimic painting, here the filming overpasses the static but retains the quality of the pictorial. The set-up's co-relation to the first sequence is clarified by the camera pausing to show us Sara's artist husband, who in a pose that matches Sara's, is astride a ladder, painting. His face is turned away completely from the audience, and his right arm is raised as he paints on the oversize canvas that covers the wall completely. The canvas, analogous to the blackboard, is as a screen here, if a little less accessible than the screen/board had been in the first sequence. Crowded or almost completed as the canvas is, it allows less room for one to enter into it, or even to let one's imagination run. When the camera swivels all the way over the artist husband Victor's head to the entrance of the room, we see a few more paintings, all with splashes of color, creating the fullness of what André Bazin called the importance of décor in film as distinct from drama: "As Jean Paul Sartre, I think it was said, in the theatre drama proceeds from the actor, in the cinema it goes from décor to man" (1967: 102). Bazin is invested in the realism of the décor that is crucial for our understanding of the complexity of human dramatic action, as in the case of the final swamp scene in Orson Welles's *Touch of Evil* (1958); however, even a scene that looks as though in part it were a painted set is served well by setting up an objective co-relative between the setting and the subject. Collins makes this connection between décor and subject for both Sara and Victor.

Enhancing the complementarity of the arts, both scenes are balanced by distance and closeness. A radio voice over brings the auditory letter into the scene; at the philosophical level, the discussion is as abstract as, if not more so than, the classroom philosophical interrogation. Victor is listening to a talk on the relationship between art and philosophy: "A whole category of philosophical problems revolve around those abstract definitions of what is or is not acceptable as art." The meta-reflexive suspension of that question is pursued by the film at the level of the diegetic interaction between characters, but also in its own filming process, contributing to the text's philosophical drive. The parity between the two sequences is not least because of the mobile camera, which as the third ever present art in the scene holds pride of place in both sequences. The latter is worth emphasizing because shifts in the use of the mobile camera not only enhance the effectiveness of the scene but also carry weight in commentary on the relationship across the pictorial, literary, and cinematic.

Borrowing from theatre where setting and blocking are crucial to the action of the play, the film develops narrative through set décor pieces but uses obvious filmic references to convey ideological and philosophical values.

A word about the derivation of this perspective on the role of the arts in film and their status in the diegesis may be helpful. In approaching silent film in terms of the "rivalry" between the arts, Brigitte Peucker evaluates each art in the hierarchy of discourses in the film, and even more fascinatingly returns to the diegesis to tie each art to a gender. Using F. W. Murnau's films, she argues that painting, the still art, is sealed by the narrative, rendering painting feminine, and narrative, usually aligned with the camera and its power to narrate, the masculine. Given that the abstract conflict in *Losing Ground* is between philosophy/literature and art/painting, and that at the level of the diegetic the tension is between a woman and a man, the connections between the diegesis and the mode of art it privileges at any point reveal the aesthetics and the ideology of the text (Peucker 1995).

That Sara as a character is closely aligned with film works at several different levels. On the one hand, the iris shot of her taken by the student would-be filmmaker, George, lingers on her as she is unaware, leading us to assume that this is a classic voyeuristic shot. In this reading, the female would be the pictorial, the male cinematic, with aesthetic values corresponding to their genders. Although the student does not have a camera, mitigating that parcel of authority, he has an old-fashioned monocle, and, in general, any extra viewing apparatus trained upon a woman is an exercise of male power. However, these neatly assigned gender values do not fall into place easily. Sara is, for instance, in her office, separated intellectually and spatially by a huge table; he is almost crouching, he is the supplicant. This very basic reading of power relations in the scene does not tell the whole story, as Collins draws our attention to film as an art form. The student compares Sara to Pearl McCormack in *The Scar of Shame*. The student wants the professor to act in his student film. Thus, the urgent plot question is reshaped: will Sara act in his film, or not? Film then has come to occupy center stage, and Sara herself is to some extent on trial to see if she will move beyond the traditional arts. As referred to earlier, *The Scar of Shame* is about a tragic mulatta, a theme that will be reprised in the student film that Sara participates in as the folk hero Frankie. And here is where those binaries of the pictorial and narrative as feminine and masculine break down altogether, as Collins, in this association between the female and the pictorial, dignifies the black female star as a great artist of the silent film era. That reference is crucial to the film; it is not merely intertextual, but acts as an active influence in the film.

The theorization about the female's pictorial values, and her consequent relegation do not appear to obtain in the diegesis as a consequence of the comparison with Pearl McCormack, who plays the bourgeois black woman. That sleight-of-hand introduction of African American film history with a complete attribution— date and name of production company: Philadelphia Colored Players, 1927—establishes the importance of its existence, and most importantly, that black women were seen and, as result of preservation efforts, can still be seen on the silver screen. The theme is further augmented by a reference to Dorothy Dandridge in the 1953 MGM film *Bright Road* (dir. Mayer). Black women playing a sympathetic role is very often an absent, magnifying the importance of McCormack's presence in a film such as *The Scar of Shame* and rendering irrelevant the pictorial = feminine = power-less in terms of ideological dispersal. Sara is now aligned with film and Pearl McCormack has effected a switch whereby the central art in the film, cinema, is gendered feminine. The question of what is "acceptable" as art, posed earlier, is answered by the radio voice over that declares the black artist's only "mandate" is to "interpret that which is real to him in a meaningful way." The answer, broad as it is, yokes black art and universalism together under the rubric of an authentic "realism," by which the commentator means that any method or mode is acceptable if the artist seeks to communicate his/her reality. The equal weight given to the painting/office sequences is consonant with Collins's stated beliefs that like McCormack, all black artists have the liberty to enact their reality the way they choose (Collins 1984a).

Setting itself becomes a matter of contention between the philosopher wife and the artist husband when he wishes to spend the summer in upstate New York. Sara comments that Victor "would like it there. It's like a painting," and says that she needs a library. The setting then is instrumental as a backdrop for both the cinematic uses of the literary and the pictorial, and their ability to offer transcendence. The low-key quarrelling about location becomes sharper when Victor jokingly says, "Would you like to put this mulatto crisis on hold?," referring back to those themes in the movies. Abstract painting, and painting, holds greater sway over him, the implication being that film is a lesser art.

The potential of each art to convey authenticity, and of black art to do so, is repeated in the discussion between the actor mother, the daughter, and the son-in-law. The mother scoffs at the plays she acts in, which fall into stereotypical black patterns: the black matriarch, her grip over the family, and her belief in God. She would rather "play a real Negro woman who thinks more about men than God." This particular dinner scene is used to convey that what we see unfold over the dinner table is real, and that if we had expected to see a predictable female role, our very expectations constrain the expansion of black female representation. The dinner scene sequence is imported from drama, the witty conversation used to entertain the audience. Bazin's comment that in drama the actors are central, the décor is not, is relevant; for this is the first time we see the two chief characters engage in social conversation. The camera is not intrusive, except for a close-up of Sara, very different than the student's "close-up." The close-up is one of very few close-ups in the film, but it does underline the cinematic art's power to reveal more than what the dialogue does; however, dramatic convention dominates, the camera follows the dialogue, spotlighting the actor when it is her turn to speak. Again, the balance between the arts is harmonious. It is also noteworthy that editing is used to commandeer the theatrical space of the dining room table for the women, Victor being out of the frame for the more serious part of the conversation. Following an earlier thread regarding gender assignations to the arts within the diegesis of a film, theatre is firmly feminized, not surprisingly, given Collins's overwhelming involvement with the arts of theatre.

Figure 6.2 *Losing Ground*: Tableau vivant

Because of the relative lack of movement of the characters, the dining room sequence could be seen as a tableau vivant. Tableaux vivants were common acts for traveling groups before the advent of cinema. The poses of the actors modeled the still painting; they then surprised the audience with their movement (Wiegand 2015). Still tableaux were very common in early twentieth-century drama too; just before the curtains were drawn the actors stood in frozen poses. The theatrical setting of the dining room, with its interpositioning of another art form associated with painting, layers the sequence even as the conversation winds backwards to Victor's sentiments about modernist art and the mother's about contemporary plays. This sequence synthesizes many of the inter-arts elements that Collins uses to provide a diegetic space for the women characters in the arts, *and* to represent their ability to inhabit and to shape them.

The dialogue across literature, painting, and film serves as a discursive vehicle to narrate the story of *Losing Ground*. In addition to including the theatre, Collins brings in dance. Dance figures in the diegesis and as film performance in the extra-diegetic. Vaudeville, as film performance in the extra-diegetic, is also folded in, almost as though to pay homage to the cavernous jaws of film that can chew and absorb it all. The dialogue, if mockingly, offers a philosophy of film and its relationship to the same elements that Victor had associated with abstract art. While rehearsing for the film within the film, Sara and Duke discuss the nature of the film, not without considerable wryness. Duke wants to know if this is an avant-garde film, to which Sara, presumably quoting the student filmmaker, says that film is about the relationship of the characters to space and light.

Two of the dance sequences between Sara and Duke are rehearsals, a third is a social dance. Sara and Victor never dance. In addition, Nellie Bly, playing the role of Frankie's competitor, dances with Duke in the extra-diegetic film and is left hanging when Frankie blows Johnny away. The chain of dizzying substitutions is also fitted in by the film, particularly with the aid of the film within the film. The dispersal of femininity across three women and one ghost woman feminizes all the arts, but not as in the early male-directed films, as passive, but as mobile, with the added virtues and abilities of the moving picture. Victor it is who is passive in the last dance sequence, but he too is granted grace, as the viewer who understands the power of art and who becomes aware of the artistic prowess of women, a revelation for the "artist" who has thought of them as models and, without putting too fine a point on it, objects of visual pleasure. In going through some of the incomplete resolutions of the film through the metafilm, the characters in the diegesis and the viewers acknowledge the moment of shock over the new, what the modernists called ostranenie, or strangeness. And in that moment, it is apparent that art is not "pure" but impure, mixed in with multiple desires and modes, conscious or unconscious; finally, that art is in the process.

Dance crosses into the extra-diegetic as among the most dynamic of the arts, for in the retelling of the Frankie and Johnny ballad, the dance tells the story, availing of literature's ability to tell a story over time, and painting's to visualize imagery in space, revealing the same capacities as the art of film. The filmic reference, the motif of the tragic mulatta, is mixed into the dance.

The harmony of the arts is suggested through an exceptional use of synesthesia in the central dance sequence in *The Cruz Brothers*. The soundtrack plays music for Miss Malloy in the clearing, being claimed for a dance first by Victor and then by José. Felipe, wandering in, literally wails for the music to stop, and it does. A synesthetic effect is created by Felipe's reaction. However, Felipe is not the only one to have "heard" the music; it is clear the other three do too, as they dance in time to the music they cannot possibly hear. The auditory is then signaled by the visual for the characters in the diegesis, and its impact experienced by the audience as synesthetic.

Collins's films provoke a synesthetic response by their rich translation of sound into sight, and vision into sound, as part of what Merleau-Ponty explained as the response of the "whole sensory being" (Szaloky 2002: 25). Collins was familiar with this phenomenological approach, arising from existentialism, philosophies that would have been central in her studies at the Sorbonne (Klotman [1982] 2015).

The characters in the diegesis while dancing respond to auditory impulses that are largely initiated by visual elements that would appear to be extraneous to sensory stimuli, the clothes, the careful movements, the gestures of the dancers following unheard melodies. The difference of course is that we hear the music. This particular form of synesthesia is to be differentiated from visual hearing; for instance, music, or audible sounds that evoke visual images. A recent example of visual hearing in the jazz music world is the Josh Lawrence Quartet, a group that evokes the painter Kandinsky's colors and form through the line of the music. The dance sequence in *The Cruz Brothers* suggests "the mental hearing of visually perceptible sounds" for the characters in the diegesis, and conveys the magical and uncanny features of the experience to us who can both hear and see, and thus are privileged to be at the juncture of the visual auditory, the aural ocular, and the complete complement of the visual and the auditory. The use of synesthesia as a technique draws our attention to how the arts produce effects in the viewer. In other words, the scene mentioned above shows the effects of synesthesia upon the characters in the diegesis. These effects are based on the viewer being what Vivian Sobchak calls "a cinesthetic subject" (Szaloky 2002: 114). The notion of the cinesthetic subject is rooted in the idea of embodied subjectivity. Countering the visuality thesis prevalent in cinema studies, Jonathan Crary argues that viewers of the Impressionist paintings were not merely interpellated as Cartesian subjects, but experienced the painting through the sensations of the body; thus, their responses to the modernity of the paintings cannot be attributed solely to the visual. The perception of one sense is received by the cinesthetic viewer through more than one sense (Crary 1999).

The Cruz Brothers and Miss Malloy addresses a cinesthetic subject, and demands that we respond to the film using both visual and sensory perceptions. Of course, it could be argued that all art works demand this response to a greater or lesser extent; however, the Collins films strive for what the 1920s european modernists called the "Gesamtkunstwerk," literally the "total art" work, but a more apt term might gesture towards synthesis in the work of art.

The opening sequence of *The Cruz Brothers* is a synthesis of auditory elements that involve several of the arts: literature, drama, music, and film. The titles in cursive, flashy, jagged writing are an acknowledgment of writing and the literary. The introductory dialogue by Victor fulfills an expository function by explaining the action, hotwiring the cars, and setting up any dramatic conflict. The literary is combined with the filmic by sound; Poppa's voice over is both a hallmark of the possibilities of sound film, but also adds a layer to the density of the narrative. Ominous cinematic sound effects imply that the easy hotwiring plan may be thwarted. And in the meanwhile, the soundtrack plays Latin music to the accompaniment of Victor in the diegesis talking to an extra-diegetic, invisible interlocutor. A loud crash of the car, followed by the young Cruz brothers running, their backs to the camera, catches the agility of movement. A dramatic pop of a gunshot marks the beginning of the auditory flashback, the visual completely suspended by the gunshot, the frame empty and blacked out for close to 20 seconds. The visual is overmatched by the auditory in this sequence; whereas in the dance sequence visual surplus leads to the auditory, here auditory surplus uses the absence of striking visual detail to interject itself as a vital element in the storytelling process, the narrative, or the literary.

The auditory, the dialogue in theatre that Collins was practiced in, is transmuted in the film where two voices engage with each other, and present asides to the audience, but the effect is fully cinematic in that the camera moves wavily along showing us the houses that Victor is talking about to his invisible father, even as he tries to get his tape machine on to record his thoughts. The two voices, the disagreement between father and son, simultaneously approximates the conflict of the theatre and the stream of consciousness of the novel, synthesized by the camera that greedily brings in the stillness of painting by capturing the pictorial qualities of the houses in the neighborhood. The inclusion of the neighborhood mixes the private with the public, the interior with the exterior, for houses in and of themselves are the central focus of the film, sites where the interior and exterior intersect.

The visual is not absolutely essential to establish presence. Victor's father is never visible, but constantly present, and also an active narrator of the film. The film uses auditory presence and absence as a powerful structuring element in the development of narrative and enhancement of mood. Victor's interiority is also revealed through the auditory, the tape machine he speaks into; his interlocutor his invisible but auditorily present father.

One of the routine functions of the soundtrack is to heighten the viewer's cinesthetic subjectivity by augmenting the emotions and sensations evoked by the diegesis of the film. The story then is enhanced. In general, the narrative function is not taken over by a piece of music in the soundtrack except in Hollywood musicals and in the song and dance sequences of the Bombay Hindi film. The narrative of the Cruz brothers is carried by a song in one of the more semiotically charged sequences of *The Cruz Brothers and Miss Malloy* when the brothers walk over the side-ropes of the bridge, a steep plunge into certain death, if there is a misstep. The song is jaunty and opens when the brothers make their way to the parks. While the object of a character's vision can be easily signaled in the film through the suturing process, one that Collins seldom uses in a straightforward way, the ability to signal what is the object of a character's hearing is not so deliberately marked, even when the source of the sound is diegetic. The song begins "We're brothers," adventuring brothers who are balancing on an impossibly slender rope with sticks, picturing the joy of their being high in the sky, the very low angles silhouetting them on the rope, first as one brother passes the danger point, and then the next. A brief dramatically close-up shot of Victor introduces the next phrase as Victor's acoustic sound picture: "But every now and then I wish / that from my father just a fewer seeds were sown." This is quickly followed by a "Hey" objecting to that line, the response even more rapid, "Just kidding." That they can hear this music almost escapes us at the moment, for we can hear it. The visual here composes the auditory, the joyful bridge crossing creating the certainty that the brothers can hear this music. Employing a technique much used in silent films such as Murnau's *Sunrise* to simulate sound effects, this sequence doubles the sound effect of both heard and unheard music. The music carries the charge of Victor's narrative of the family, adding another narrative layer to his thoughts as he records them on his tape. The shot that links Victor's interiority to the viewer's visual and auditory functions as a sound suture between the auditory spectator and the character, Victor in the diegesis constructing both Victor and the auditory spectator as cinesthetic subjects of the visual and the aural.

The inter-arts pattern can also be discerned in the uses to which nature is pressed in the film. The landscape is no mere cinematographic backdrop, and several shots are exclusively of natural scenes. These have the quality of romantic landscape paintings, but also an aura of desolation, as though their beauty, starkly contrasted to the shack the brothers live in, belongs to others. These shots of the landscape are strangely disconnected from the characters except in the most cursory of contrasts with the Bronx. Yet, the shots of the lotus pond and the lush greenness have narrative weight in that they reveal a different world to the brothers, starting with the misty early morning walk to Miss Malloy's house. Despite the overall soft focus of this sequence, the aesthetic of the landscape is strangely distant except in the sequences filled with action, as when the brothers tumble in the grass to get to the hoop. The dance sequence in the green, discussed earlier, when Felipe explodes, illustrates the uneasy relationship between the seemingly un-giving landscape and the brothers. Nevertheless, the inertness of the landscape is animated by the brothers working on it for Miss Malloy, chopping, carrying, cleaning in the dense woods, their abilities gainsaying the indifference of the landscape. The soundtrack through the approach is slow, intermittent, and serves as announcements of their making their way into the property. In these sequences, the characters themselves are pictures—still. When the brothers are first greeted by Miss Malloy, they could be a tableau in a set, she a talking full-length picture, both groups brought to size by the landscape. Several other sequences, such as when the brothers work in the grounds, convey the same quality of an estrangement that is marvelous.

The inter-arts approach that Collins takes has its broadest base in what Teshome Gabriel claims black artists share with nomads, the belief in "collective memory" and the commonality of language: "symbolism, metaphor, music performance" (Gabriel 2001: 402). The collective memory in both films is brought in by the symbolism of the ancestral trace (Poppa in *Cruz Brothers* and vaudun in *Losing Ground*), by the metaphor of the cinema in both films, the soundtrack with its diegetic overtones in the *Cruz Brothers*, and finally the dances in both films.

7

Black feminist culture and black masculinity

Collins's work has cleared new ground for the visual in African American culture as seen in the increasingly urgent demands of critics that all artistic practices, especially film, be rooted in the larger African American culture (Gillespie 2016). By including painting and literature as integral components of the visual, *The Cruz Brothers* and *Losing Ground* succeed in locating black/minority individuals engaged in the business of discovering the value of art in life.

In her screenplays and dramas, Collins identifies the many existential issues that confront black men and women in their interactions with each other even as they try to find fulfillment in creative pursuits. The emphasis on the interior life impinges on philosophies of identities where blackness jostles with the human exigencies of finding a community without yielding the continuing search for a core self. These writings lay out the design for the essai films.

"Women, Sisters, and Friends," a film script written in 1971, a decade before Collins was to make her films, belongs to this category, where blackness is not unitary and confining but universal and, in that sense, belonging to "world literature." The script features women conversing about intransigent men that they are attracted to, only to find fulfillment elusive. The texts imply, in both major and minor keys, that completeness is to be sought in artistic and intellectual endeavors. The theme is patently followed in *Losing Ground*, and to a lesser extent in *Cruz Brothers*.

The script of "Women, Sisters, and Friends" has an expressionistic and surrealistic tinge to it. The visionary impulse of Expressionist poetry and drama is apparent in the allegorical depiction of the man coming in from the sea. The script is not tightly plotted, but roams across the women's desires, their histories, their presents, their pasts. The screenplay already evinces some of the aesthetic patterns and themes Collins would return to in her plays and films—the contrast between the exterior and interior mise-en-scènes—the exterior animated by movement and action and very often dream-like, the interior a place to converse endlessly about life, art, people, sex, self, emotions. All her work has at least one scene or sequence where women talk to each other freely. That space she sought to create for women to talk about their lives, as distinct from their being represented, is still rare in film and drama today in its high seriousness and in its complete affirmation of women's thinking. Seldom does one see such interchanges centered. Two shifts occur as a consequence of this recurrent trope: both whiteness and masculinity do not function any longer as inevitable reference points; the women's exchange of ideas serves as the ultimate linguistic code.

Organized around three women and their accounts of their life experiences, the script uses off-screen dialogue and commentary to deflect the visual in a slow subversive but undefined mockery of the natural beauty of the setting, the beach. Female desire is presented nakedly; one of the women, Marita, wants to wander out on the beach at 3 a.m. hoping for an encounter with an unnamed man who is known to walk around there. The man is cast in terms of Oskar Kokoschka's men in "Murderer, Hope of Women" in the elemental presentation, but is Laurentian in the male surrender to women. The female language of desire emerges in this script, to be refined in many other scripts and plays, but is fully expressed in surmounting sexual desire while grasping at an essentially indescribable tenderness. Lillie, talking to herself, reminisces about a man who had told her of his first time with a woman: "He was so overcome that he held out his penis to her as an offering, his face weeping" (Collins 1971). The image of his "face" weeping instead of him weeping is deft in capturing the immensity of the moment. Collins uses just such images in the concluding scene of *Losing Ground* when the faces of both Sara and Victor are equally transparent. We see another cinematic variant when Felipe, Victor's brother, accosts his brothers dancing with Miss Malloy in *Cruz Brothers*.

Replete with elements of the marvelous real, within the specific context of the African diaspora, "Women, Sisters, and Friends" introduces a motif that Collins's films would later develop. In the script, an old woman enters the scene and, with a silent Lillie for an audience, starts recounting the tale of her younger sister's almost otherworldly coupling with her lover, and then her death. The old woman's appearance in the script is ephemeral and mysterious, and her voice announces her before she is visible. She could well be an ancestral presence that has been summoned. The otherworldly is thrown into relief by the reference to the broken bottles that the sister used to make objects of art, puzzling for the old woman. In Gullah culture, bottles and pots that belonged to people who had died were retained to keep their spirits alive, and although the old woman does not appear to know this, she keeps the bottles her sister has left behind. Traces of otherworldliness are manifest in *Cruz Brothers* in the presence of the ghost in the machine, Poppa, and in *Losing Ground* in the psychic's hints, as also in the description of the vaudun rituals. The script has other motifs that are central to African/African American culture; for example, a wedding procession with a sermon on marriage and love, except that this one is excerpted from Rainer Maria Rilke's "Letters to a Young Poet"; and a folk tale about a young mulatto girl whom everyone mistrusted, even her lover, so that she walked away to meet the god of the sea, which touches upon an old motif of the slaves walking into the water to resist white oppression. Here, it is the girl who is struggling against "colorism" in the community, and gender stereotypes because of her beauty. The script touches on the antagonistic aspects of masculinity as well as the more sympathetic. One of the three women, Marita, returns from her uncle's funeral—time is completely ignored in the script—and defends her uncle's terrible weakness, no willpower to transcend the "sickness," the burden of representing the race at all times enforced by class status. A spiritual accompanies the cultural material in the script, further adding to the performative elements that were to be staples of Collins's movies. Many of the ideas in this script, the atmosphere, the richness of exchange among the women, who discuss whether they have come or not, is not translated in either of her films except by extreme indirection, and very glancingly, even that coming in for criticism for its lack of verisimilitude.

The screenplays and scripts reveal the repertoire of techniques Collins would later translate into film practice. Sound usage in these writings carries over into the films. Almost all her works, including *Cruz Brothers*, have several off-screen dialogues that denaturalize both the dialogue and the setting. Off-screen sound would appear to have a will of its own, and is more than slightly apart from the visual scene and its cues. Part of such dialogue is to emphasize the language of thought and emotion; to listen to it, instead of having it emoted. In feminist film theory, starting with Arzner criticism, critics have traced the techniques feminist directors use to conceal the private emotions of women, too often the sensational allure of mainstream film. In "Women, Sisters, and Friends," Sylvia, one of the characters, is overheard by us, as she engages in a long phone conversation with a man, George, whom she tries to persuade, with no success, to come and visit her. The dialogue alone lets us know that Sylvia is alternately placating, threatening, and feeling helpless and angry at the same time over a quasi-daily undramatic encounter. The tail end of the one-sided conversation gives us a fairly full view of Sylvia's emotions about George, given that the women are in a location that they think offers them plenitude and grace: "Oh, George, you can't really not be coming because your library books are due on Monday" (Collins 1971). Telephone conversations, a device to connect the action to a different theatre, occur frequently, functioning as an abstract theatrical substitute for the more conventional cinematic parallel editing.

The screenplay mixes the pictorial, the literary, the performative, and the cinematic, combining the mundane, the magical, and the metaphysical in the narrative. The metaphysical joins with the literary and performative when one of the other women, Lillie, comes down the misty beach talking to herself, telling of how a man had told her of his first time when he was sixteen. There is an unashamed admiration for the male body, that verges on the discovery of one's own body through another: "He stood there and as I was watching him I became slowly aware of how completely at ease he was inside his own body, turned towards some private moment all his own" (Collins 1971). Lillie's memory, narrated, conjures up the pictorial with the weight of her awareness of the sacred erotic, and his sheer wonder about passion. Of equal importance is that this section is a revelation of interiority, of a kind of stream of consciousness that is modernist, but also surreal in bringing in the possibility of the consciousness/unconscious of three people. The screenplay is quite avant-garde, anti-narrative, and describes desire, fantasy, and reality in modes that are not obsessively marked but does show what Irigaray would call "a women's language," even where there are clear signs of Kokoschka in the atavistic longing of the women for the man (Irigaray 1985b). The screenplay also makes the switch from recording the male unconscious to the female in contrast to Dulac's *The Seashell and the Clergyman* (1928). The films that Collins eventually completed have some of these elements but are more tightly wound in a narrative, more so in *Cruz Brothers* than in *Losing Ground*.

Another screenplay, "Lila" (1974), is of particular interest to *Losing Ground* as it is a raw treatment of the ego of the male artist. Featuring an artistic couple—Ben, a drummer, and Marita, a television producer—the screenplay follows the volatile impulses of Ben. Ben creates playful but aggressive scenarios for them to enact; Marita plays along but drops the role to Ben's disdain. Playacting is psychically threatening for the female here but is radically reshaped in *Losing Ground* where the female acts to further a deeper psychic connection with herself.

"Lila" substantively anticipates the exploration of the differences between manifestations of male and female creativity examined in *Losing Ground*. Ben, like Victor, claims artistic license to be unfaithful and is cavalier about his girlfriend Marita's devotion to him. He meets a woman who is both remarkably naïve and almost unearthly in her physical perfection, Alice. She is mundane in her preoccupations and is mired in an ordinary, difficult existence, one that Ben ignores. The screenplay is darker about the male artist's role when Ben begins to use her as a model. He grooms Alice, manipulating her with his greater awareness of the world. The Pygmalion motif is stronger here than it is either in *Losing Ground* or in *The Cruz Brothers*. Ben purposefully changes Alice's name to Lila, very obviously "remaking" her in his own divine, artistic image. Victor projects similar fantasies on Celia, the Puerto Rican dancer he uses as a model, calling her "Celia Cruz," but Celia in *Losing Ground* is quite resistant and opposes Victor's delusions of artistic grandeur.

In "Lila," Ben drags Alice into acting out scenarios that are supposedly wild, but Alice's story is wilder. Reality confronts art in a manner that Ben is quite incapable of absorbing. When they are in the Museum of Modern Art in New York, Alice suddenly points to a painting depicting a man with an axe, indexically of her father, who had brought an axe down on her mother's head. More nonplussing are the details that follow, of how her mother now has to wear her hair as an Afro all the time to cover the long gash. Ben's subterranean violent tendencies are revealed at the level of language when, straight after this scene, he insists on scraping Alice's hair back, despite her strenuous objections, and pinning it up; a further reshaping of her, less in terms of an ideal, more cynical, deliberately indulging an unspoken violence, covered up by notions of modernist artistic freedoms and the language that accompanies them. Collins strongly objects to the male artistic debasement of modernism's ideals when it comes to women in extraordinarily strong terms in this screenplay, a theme she follows in *Losing Ground*. The difference appears to be that both women, Alice, and Marita, despite her professional accomplishments, seem powerless to oppose Ben: Alice because she is out of her depth, and Marita because she loves him. The women are linked to each other, and to a stylish female model that surfaces in one of the scenes. Marita fantasizes about being the photographer's model, dressing up in velvet pants. Another scene makes the link between the photographer's model, the artist's model, Alice, and the TV producer would-be photographer's model, Marita. Ben "dresses up" Alice, who is delighted with the velvet pants, much as a child would be with playing dress-up. Alice invites her friends to come and watch her, unknowingly subverting Ben's fantasies by rendering them commonplace among her working friends, teachers, hospital employees, service workers, all of whom Ben finds irrelevant. The connection made between the women here suggests that they are all interchangeable, and in that sense, does not quite rise to doubling, although there are hints of it in Marita's brief fantasy of being an artist's model. In *Losing Ground*, the doubling of women is infinitely more enriching to the women themselves, as the folding of the double into the self is based on the women's discovery of an otherness worth inviting.

In many of her writings, Collins presents clusters of women's communities within the larger social network to suggest that these relationships support black women in their efforts to retain a sense of themselves as independent, creative people. The writings are framed by the efforts of the characters to live in a world where art matters and where it is taken seriously as work, and where the female's authority over her self and her work guides her life. Without fail, Collins's work takes women's eroticism seriously and follows the damages wrought to women when their desires remain unarticulated and when, inevitably, they are not fulfilled. Race is imbricated subtly in this theme where the author/dramatist shows that the relationships between black women and men are deeply damaged by an awareness of blackness as a psychic flaw. Even as the characters may recognize that the psychic wounds have been internalized because of the social imaginary and they willfully seek to negate them, the women particularly find that the men have greater difficulty understanding how their brokenness affects them and their relationships with women.

The screenplay "A Summer Diary" (n.d.) treats male difficulties with racial and gender identity. It uses writing, a recurring trope, to foreground the interiority of black subjects (Collins 2019). The text describes a modest effort at a women's community when two women, Caroline and Lilianne, with their children decide to live together. The editing in the screenplay, as in the bulk of Collins's work, links the lives of women and invites the audience to make comparisons between them. Collins suggests that in their individual experiences, a universal black feminist theme is apparent: of the impossibility of being black and female; and being black and female and striving to own a creative project is in and of itself devastating.

The directions in "A Summer Diary" are characteristic of Collins's style. She uses medium wide shots very often to introduce characters, and a stationary camera to capture their conversations. She seldom uses shot/reverse shot, part of her investment in not "manipulating" her characters. Discussions on the shot/reverse shot technique maintain that the rapid eye movement of the viewer would veer towards one character or the other, and hence shot/reverse shot would imitate the "natural." Detractors claim that the rapidity of the cutting allows access to the emotions of only one character, thus coercing the viewer. From a feminist stylistic framework, shot/reverse shot is theorized as intrusive of the female character; the medium wide shot without cuts allows for a more nuanced understanding of the context. The screenplay's use of female voice overs is also a staple of feminist narratology, primarily to counter a history of authoritative male voice overs. The expository function of the voice over is crucial in specifying the narrative course of action and lending credibility to the events. In "A Summer Diary," Caroline informs us of the death of Lilianne's husband, Gilles. Although having committed suicide the summer before, Gilles appears as a jaunty ghost quite often in the house; Caroline's voice over serves as an introduction of a member of the cast in a play. The ghost motif recurs in *The Cruz Brothers and*

Miss Malloy, another instance of the African diaspora ancestral motif that would be drawn out in Julie Dash's *Daughters of the Dust* (1991). The idea of haunting hints at lingering debts the living owe the dead; while offering tokens for ancestors are ritualized in African culture, in Collins's work the ghosts seem to be bearing witness to the living, and urging them to deserve the lives they have, wages for the struggles of the dead.

Much of the dialogue in the screenplays dwells on artistic projects and aspirations. Collins brings in arts as diverse as weaving and sculpting, photography and playwriting, set-design and instrumental music into her scripts almost as though to cover the spectrum of possibilities for black artists and craft workers. Put together, her works compose a group portrait of the black artist with the black female artist at the center. The world of art that she depicts, although replete with creative exuberance, is quite often dark and chaotic, particularly for women artists. "A Summer Diary" reveals a more violent aspect associated with the arrogance of the male artist, a casual callousness exceeding indifference. Caroline tells Lilianne of her husband Rafael's photographic model, who pulls a knife on Caroline; Rafael dismisses the episode as the belly dancer's temperament, almost blaming Caroline for not having the same frenzied temperament.

Each of Collins's works is marked by a meta-reflective episode of considerable length. While these are elaborated in multiple modalities in her two films, her screenplays also have this component, whereby the characters in the diegesis and in the audience are treated to an entertainment set. "A Summer Diary" features singing, a frequent occurrence in much of her work, and a fairly fleshed-out musical drama, complete with the director giving the chorus instructions on character and acting profiles. The screenplays themselves are constructed episodically, setting almost no stock on the action but throwing the weight on the emotional unrolling of the female characters. Flashbacks in both "A Summer Diary" and "Women, Sisters, and Friends" fill in the gaps to contextualize the women's emotional stances. The work of art within the artefact is proof of its production, carrying the traces of the work instrumental in assembling it. To a large extent, the work of art then is demystified, and exposed for its relentless demands of energy and work. The characters are often shown doing battle with the everyday problems of an artist on the rise. The social circle can be equally chilly. When Caroline in "A Summer Diary" tells her father of a script on a woman and her attempts to understand her feelings on love, she is almost shamefaced, anticipating his skepticism. After all, he has designated her profession, set-designing, amorphous and lacking character. Yet, the play within the screenplay, or the film within the film, or the dance within the film are triumphant in the moment of achievement, and inspiring to the implied audience in the texts.

"Almost Music: A Cabaret Play" (1980) with music by Michael Minard, who would score the music for *Cruz Brothers*, reflects on song, its allure and its falseness. The perils and pleasures of romance recall the fleeting sentiments of pathos, the provenance of the "Negro" music offering another note of melancholy not rendered. The cabaret artists, characters longing to experience life in a sharper way, quite purely seek love. The female characters are girl-women, quite unlike the characters in Collins's plays and films. A chorus of women drinkers serve as filters to the action of the play, an implied audience who have traversed this path and raucously support the female singer in her need to sing of love, a theme that the piano player adamantly opposes. Sex is okay, so is politics; war is acceptable; but love, that is the kiss of death, no one will feel good with songs of love and its bleeding messes. The interruptions from the piano player, the screaming of the chorus of women even as the female singer vaguely reminisces with a man, identified only as such, shift spectating positions dramatically as women viewers throw their lot in with the chorus of women, and then are compelled to a more social stance by the forms of music, rather than the underlying emotions. The strategy is post-expressionist in showing both the veneer and the raw primal emotion beneath. The singer and the chorus of women are not naïve romantics; rather, they are ironic, and pained about their longings and about the refusal of conventional art to give voice to these. The singer confides in the women about male anger, incomprehensible to her after an evening of pleasure; a stinging rejection as the man takes off to any which place in the dead of the night. And this happens, not once, but three different times, leaving the singer semi-catatonic in pain. The language of music here once again recalls feminist efforts to speak a different language, one that is not stuck in Aristotelian dicta. The songs become darker through the cabaret, moving from longing to desperation; the music and art become ways of holding the self together. For women, to aspire to love and to be modern is shown to be a contradiction in terms. And yet, whether in an anguished or semi-droll register, the singer is not willing to give it up. Proper names are not ascribed to any of the characters, augmenting the expressionist impulse, given to allegory and referring to the universal. The play closes cursorily, open-ended, and comes back callously to the conventions of the genre, revealing cynically the shabby cover-up of art in throwing it all back at the audience.

"In the Midnight Hour," a play written in 1978 and published in 1980, is about the dangers of upper-class blacks burying all consciousness of race to attempt to live life freely without race expectations dogging them. The play could easily be mistakenly regarded as a Woody Allen rough script featuring characters shooting the breeze, gently mocking each other while musing about themselves. The conversation skirts around the edges, fear of exteriors and facades holding sway. Unlike Genet's "The Blacks" (1959) that reveals characters playing a conscious double game with both themselves and white society, or Edward Albee's "Who's Afraid of Virginia Woolf?" (1962) that tears the strips off any exterior modeling of the psyche, the characters in this play crumble, trying to avoid any conscious acknowledgment of race and its impact on their identities. The dramatist subtly locates them in black culture; she mixes media effortlessly in her work—in this case, music. The characters spend an evening on the Westside of New York listening to three versions of "Take the A Train," the train to Harlem and the black community, by Duke Ellington, Anita O'Day, and Carmen McCrae. Ornette Coleman is also played while the deliberateness of the New York cosmopolitan life, ultimately at odds with the universalist, is emphasized. Christine, one of the visitors to the middle-class Abernathy apartment, is a Barnard girl brought home by the seemingly radiant young adult children of the family. All three youngsters are on the verge of joining a "reform," a political action movement. The superhuman effort is to persuade the next generation that being black in the US is not destructive. Ralph, the father, mock-proudly states that there were "No negro reasons ruining [his] life" (Collins [1980] 2002: 31), a low-key refrain punctuating the daughter's search for ecstasy, a motif through Collins's work. The bohemian friends, a piano player and a rejected would-be priest, also seek ecstasy. The piano player's route is through an insatiable haptic attachment to the keys of the piano; the failed priest's through what he labels "Religion and the Ecstatic Experience." The playwright pokes a hole in this fragile cosmopolitan caul in the bloodiest manner: the son kills himself, the father spends years chronically depressed, the mother, like many of Collins's women, is described as "drifting." The question posed by the play when the son, Ben, exclaims that he did not know who he was until he was fifteen, is whether a cosmopolitan veneer over a deeper universalist drive is possible without being sedimented in history. The issue of who one is at the cosmopolitan "party" niveau is quirky, entertaining, and self-indulgent but explodes when that who, translated as a raced interpellation, blocks all access to subjectivity. The very thin individuality of these characters forecloses any entrance to subjectivity. The father's male identity as the patriarch is demolished when these events occur and he is left with the horrifying realization of what he has done to his son. He offers his son a bare-boned apology, "Didn't tell him [the son] what was going on outside" (Collins [1980] 2002: 27).

Outside and inside serve as key determinants of identity in "The Brothers," which unblinkingly scrutinizes the destructive consequences to composing male and female identities when the outside deforms an imperceptible folded self that is barely noticeable but whose existence is felt. Set in 1948 but written during the post-civil rights era (1981), the play is about masculinity and, more specifically, about a ravaged masculinity killing women. Historical occurrences are mentioned, particularly the markers of Gandhi's assassination in 1948 and Martin Luther King Jr.'s in 1968, that suggest a Lukácsian "critical realist" orientation showing characters embedded in the historical and acting as agents in history. Collins has reversed this classic mode of locating class to show how very consciously the African American upper/upper middle class attempts to remove itself from the historical. One strategy that is used revolves around the effort to be part of the "firsts" among coloreds, another devolves to creating a refined, rarefied ambiance, but both are compelled by a Kristevan impulse to expel the abject, or at least to wage war on it. The abject is the sensory, the physical, the tangible of blackness.

Collins's screenplays and her films diverge quite sharply from any mainstream depictions of African American female sexuality, offering her black female audience and the larger public a world that popular culture does not believe exists. The representation of black sexuality whether male or female is never rendered with the richness of the intimate gaze, with the fullness of a human desire for closeness and pleasure that is revealed in *Losing Ground*, in the protagonist's understanding of her desires and her sexual relationship with her husband. Collins implies that to get to any depth, culturally toxic layers have to be shed, but that a notional racial identity lingers, disallowing any authentic acceptance of the sexual self. The denial of corporeality, the expulsion of physicality, would seem to be necessary to be "civilized," for which sexuality would need to be obviated. The problem then lies not just in the movies, but also in the cultural reification of black sexuality. A short story entitled "Stepping Back" delicately shows the war against sexuality. The woman in the story mocks herself for not being sexually eager: "As if all forms of cultural underdevelopment had somehow passed [her] by" (Collins 2016: 87). As the colored woman and man revel in each other's avoidance of the overtly sexual, the female protagonist is compelled in strongly essentialist terms by the demands of her physical body:

> My breasts stung and I longed to feel his fingers pull at them. Instead I caught myself stepping back ... retreating ... In the face of our delicacy, our ... how could I occupy the splendid four-poster bed? Tastefully enough. How could I pass beneath the candelabras and undress? Tastefully enough? No colored woman could. No colored woman could. (Collins 2016: 91)

Note the hesitation in the repetition of "tastefully enough," this time emphasized by the question mark at the end followed by the resolute repetition that "No colored woman could." The phrase repeated three times suggests that the protagonist's femininity is held hostage by the inhibitions of a notional race that obviates her sexuality and makes it other than "tasteful" or "civilized."

Mainstream film magnifies this cultural imaginary of the hyper-sexualized black subject by parlaying black sexuality through the white heteronormative male gaze in the case of the black man. The black woman's sexuality is brokered through both the white man and the black man. This phenomenon in mainstream film has its roots in the Hays Code and the archetypal patterns established by Griffith's *Birth of a Nation*. Through her analysis of *Lethal Weapon* (dir. Donner, 1987), *Colors* (dir. Hopper, 1988), and *Angel Heart* (dir. Parker, 1987), Jacquie Jones maintains that Hollywood refuses to give black men a love interest for fear of humanizing them. This "denormalizing" is the consequence of a continuous treatment of black men as "overly developed and animal forms" (Jones 1993: 249). Using psychoanalytic theory, Jones argues that black female sexuality becomes an element to be dominated by black men assuming the role of white men with black women. In discussing the relay of looks in a film such as *Mahogany* (dir. Gordy, 1975), Jane Gaines (1990) establishes a clear hierarchy whereby the black woman is subject to the gaze of the white man, white woman, black man. The black woman cannot return the look. Collins upends this hierarchy in *Losing Ground* by bypassing the relevance and power of the look and granting the female authority through control of her intellect and her sexuality.

While black masculinity was explored in a multi-faceted way by black male directors in the 1980s in the New Realism films, the representation of black women continued to remain "denormalized." Using two of the most popular of these films, Singleton's *Boyz N the Hood* (1991) and Lee's *Jungle Fever* (1991), Michele Wallace roundly charges the films with "demoniz[ing] black family sexuality as a threat to black male heterosexual identity" (Wallace 1993a: 130). The films' critique of single mothers is in line with the infamous Moynihan Report (1965) that blamed Black America's wage and achievement gap on households headed by women. Wallace's own conclusion is that there were some "alarming trend[s]" noticeable in these films, primary among them that "Black women filmmakers, not to mention black feminist film criticism were becoming unimaginable" (Wallace 1993a: 122). It is in this context that Collins wrote the scripts for her films, found financing, and shot both *Cruz Brothers* and *Losing Ground*, featuring themes and ideas about black women and colored men that were reflective, alternative, and offered ways of thinking of difference outside of the black male framework, one that effectively ejected black women from an imagined national imaginary.[1] White nationalism has lent the term national imaginary itself sinister resonances, but it is relevant at the representational level to Collins's efforts to uncover and tell the stories of people without submerging them in categories that essentially set them apart from the nation as an imagined community. Her rearticulation of masculinity to introduce "bois" that "signifies another form of masculinity" (Harris 2006: 1) with some apprehension of the universal enabled men to be participants in the social, revealing what Collins might call their "symbolic" motivation, as distinct from their "real," that pits them against the social fabric (Collins 1984a).

Collins's achievement in "normalizing" black sexuality cannot be overstated. As late as 2009, black feminist critics continued to write about the reification of black male and female sexuality on screen. The hyper-violence and hyper-sexualization of black masculinity in mainstream film persists (Mask 2009). It is instructive to consider whether the treatment of black women in the history of independent black cinema is substantially different. Independent black cinema has its beginnings in race films. Race films originated in the early part of the twentieth century because of massive African American migration to the urban north. The black bourgeoisie, which was quite substantial in cities such as Philadelphia, sought to educate the black migrants, who were not held together by the precepts of the church or by the dominant influence of local newspapers. Race films fulfilled a very important function in that they addressed a black audience, thus providing entertainment for blacks, rather than about them. Many of the vaudeville films did not necessarily engage in the "uplift" that the black middle class might have aspired to, and featured mixed-genre films that attempted to please different groups of people. *The Scar of Shame* (1927) is a preeminent example of the silent era melodramas that were essentially sociological in approach and used some of the staple figures of African American literature such as the tragic mulatto (Cripps 2003). The film features violent and exploitative men of the working classes and unappreciative, class-bound men of the upper classes. Thus, while some standard archetypes of black women were "animalistic," black independent films created black female heroes, modeled on white female heroes, who alone represented "true womanhood" (Carby 1987). Many of these race films, including the vast Micheaux corpus, show virtuous women attempting to be useful members of the community, the church, and the nation.

Collins's references to Dorothy Dandridge and Pearl McCormack indicate her admiration for these actors, particularly Dorothy Dandridge, who played the "tragic mulatto" more than once. *Carmen Jones* (dir. Preminger, 1954), starring Dorothy Dandridge, functions as a cultural trace in *Losing Ground* and shows the female seeker as doomed. In African American literature, the image of a desiring woman emerges in the Harlem

Renaissance of the 1920s and in the novels of Nella Larsen, after a long stint of women characters in literature bound to the strictures of the "cult of true womanhood." It is plausible that Helga Crane in Larsen's novel *Quicksand* (1928) is allowed to explore her sexuality because of the context of film culture, including African American films that were rewriting the tragic mulatto/a archetype. For instance, Oscar Micheaux, in his films, used visual stratagem to express female desire obliquely through dreams, flashbacks, and embedded stories. Like Micheaux, Collins uses the extra-diegetic to present women's desires, if much more forcefully and directly.

Collins was making her films after a slew of Hollywood films that featured hyper-sexualized black males and females, to the exclusion of black desiring subjectivities, whether male or female. Hollywood studios had capitalized on Melvin Van Peebles's *Sweet Sweetback's Baadasssss Song* (1971), a black urban independent film that effectively ended the era of the "vanilla" comedies starring Sidney Poitier (Guerrero 2002). Critics are divided about the contribution of Blaxploitation films; however, many, including Samuel Jackson and Quentin Tarantino, felt that these films, particularly *Shaft* (dir. Parks, 1971), allowed the black man to stride through the streets of New York as though he owned it, enhanced by the cinematography, particularly the diagonals in *Shaft* as Richard Roundtree crosses the street in the iconic opening sequence. The comment of an older black woman reminiscing about *Sweet Sweetback's Baadasssss Song* is telling in that she remembers that she and the audience were stunned and thrilled that the black character had not died, that he had actually survived at the resolution of the film (Guerrero 2002). However, while black masculinity may have been a particularly vibrant response to the Uncle Tom archetype of the Poitier films, the black buck and the Jezebel trope are repackaged affirmatively, particularly the gun-toting mama. Collins held no truck with these movies; her own reading of the power of sexuality is in a different register, more in tune with the deep human needs of her male and female characters.

Among her contemporaries, Collins appreciated Charles Burnett's *Killer of Sheep* (1977), its aesthetic, and its approach to interiority, but had reservations about his portrayal of women. Indeed, the film is avant-garde; but its great achievement, expressing the rich interior life of the black man, leaves no room for the black woman, who is pushed further and further away towards the edges of his existence. Suffice it to say that the kind of full portrayal we have of Sara in *Losing Ground* is the first of its kind in the post-civil rights era, and probably in the history of African American film.

Note

1   The cinematographer of the two films, Ronald Gray, recounts difficulties of finding financing and of completing both films in the special features section of *Losing Ground*.

Afterword

In the context of African American film studies, where accurate or "authentic" representations have been an ideal, and realism normative, Kathleen Collins shifted to offering perspectives of black/minority life outside of obvious realistic parameters. The "otherworldly" or mystical illusions provides a clearing ground for universal dialogue, connecting the interior to the exterior. In this vision of the dialogic, she interjects the philosophical to preempt any dogmatic principles from governing human action and thought.

The introduction of race into philosophic inquiry about being, the self, and the other is an attempt to underscore the processes of thinking. From the opening sequence of *Losing Ground* we see this investment in understanding the history of ideas, particularly the notion that raced subjects have been cast outside the normal, as extraordinarily lacking in virtue. Above all else, the film reveals both protagonists, not as projections of the white imaginary, but as human beings struggling with these issues while pursuing philosophy, art, and virtue.

Collins was not entirely alone in this search for a new language for African American film. Part of the New York Black Independents, she, like Gunn, used literature as a trope in the film, and translated its facility with metaphor and metonymy in her films, particularly in the use of her mise-en-scènes. Take, for instance, the landscape in *Cruz Brothers*, implacable, but in and of itself offering a glimpse into another world.

The possibility of that other world impinging on this one characterizes both *Cruz Brothers* and *Losing Ground*. The films are distinctive in offering what can only be called secular grace. No one is called to a strict accounting, none of the characters is manipulated to arrange a neat ending; we know how ideas have helped them "evolve in the center of their being" (Collins 1984a).

As ideas are shared, and animate all the characters, the world views of the film are consequently complete and communal, rather than individualistic. Collins's strategy in both films is to register the authority of a range of characters in the diegesis.

The films are modernist, countervailed by the mythical and the marvelous real in *Cruz Brothers* and amplified by the metafilmic in *Losing Ground*. Color, sound, and cinematography distinguish between the magical real and the marvelous real in *Cruz Brothers*, the aesthetics revealing the director's politics.

The repercussions for the larger community are apparent in the techniques of doubling that *Losing Ground* purveys, paying homage to black women in the African American tradition, and respecting the use value of ancestral knowledge for the contemporary black woman.

Emphasizing the artistry of the black/minority subject, the films take an integrated approach to the literary and performing arts, including dance, drama, set-design, literature, painting, and film. The aesthetic of the films is derived from this inter-arts approach.

Collins's visionary idea of locating the filmic in the larger cultural tradition emerges from her work as a writer of fiction, drama, and screenplays. This corpus establishes black women as artists, and black communities as integral to the creation of art. Countering the persistence of the racial imaginary in representations of black subjects, *The Cruz Brothers and Miss Malloy* and *Losing Ground* present worlds where black feminist culture is a reality.

Bibliography

Alexander, Elizabeth (2004), *The Black Interior*, Saint Paul, MN: Graywolf Press.
Althusser, Louis (1971), "Ideology and Ideological State Apparatuses (Notes Towards an Investigation)," in *Lenin and Philosophy and Other Essays*, trans. Ben Brewster, London: Monthly Press.
Badley, Linda, Claire Perkins, and Michele Schreiber (eds.) (2016), *Indie Reframed: Women's Filmmaking and Contemporary American Independent Cinema*, Edinburgh: Edinburgh University Press.
Baker Jr., Houston A. (1993), "Spike Lee and the Commerce of Culture," in *Black American Cinema*, ed. Manthia Diawara, New York: Routledge, an AFI Paperback.
Barthes, Roland (1994), *S/Z, Oeuvres Complètes: Tome II 1966–73*, Paris: Editions du Seuil.
Bazin, André (1967), *What is Cinema?*, Vol. 1, trans. Hugh Gray, Berkeley: University of California Press.
Bennett, Michael, and Vanessa Dickerson (eds.) (2001), *Recovering the Black Female Body: Self-Representations by African American Women*, New Brunswick: Rutgers University Press.
Benston, Kimberly (2000), *Performing Blackness: Enactments of African American Modernism*, New York: Routledge.
Beverly, Michele P. (2012), "Phenomenal Bodies: The Metaphysical Possibilities of Post-Black Film and Visual Culture," Dissertation, Georgia State University, <http://scholarworks.gsu.edu/communication_diss/37> (last accessed June 28, 2019).
Black Camera (2018), "Close-up," Vol. 9, No. 2: 6–8.
Bobo, Jacqueline [1991] (2017), "'The Subject is Money': Reconsidering the Black Film Audience as a Theoretical Paradigm," *Black American Literature Forum*, Vol. 25, No. 2: 421–32, reprinted in *African American Review*, Vol. 50, No. 4: 839–50.

Bogle, Donald (1973), *Toms, Coons, Mulattoes, Mammies and Bucks: An Interpretive History of Blacks in American Film*, New York: Bantam Books.

Bordwell, David (1996), "Convention, Construction, and Cinematic Vision," in *Post-Theory: Reconstructing Film Studies*, eds. David Bordwell and Noel Carroll, Madison: University of Wisconsin Press.

Bowser, Pearl, Jane Gaines, and Charles Musser (eds.) (2001), *Oscar Micheaux and His Circle: African American Filmmaking and Race Cinema of the Silent Era*, Bloomington: Indiana University Press.

Brody, Richard (2019), "Kathleen Collins's Notes from a Black Woman's Diary Contains an Extraordinary Unmade Movie," *The New Yorker*, February 2, <https://www.newyorker.com/culture/the-front-row/kathleen-collins-notes-from-a-black-womans-diary-contains-an-extraordinary-unmade-movie> (last accessed June 28, 2019).

Carby, Hazel (1987), *Reconstructing Womanhood: The Emergence of the Afro-American Novelist*, Oxford: Oxford University Press.

Carpentier, Alejo (2006), "On the Marvelous Real in America (1949)," in *Magical Realism: Theory, History, Community*, eds. Lois Parkinson Zamora and Wendy Faris, Durham, NC: Duke University Press. Lecture delivered late 1920s.

Cassel, Valerie (2002), "New Diaspora Artists," <http://new.diaspora-artists.net/display_item.php?id=740&table=artefacts> (last accessed June 28, 2019).

Cheah, Pheng, and Bruce Robbins (eds.) (1998), *Cosmopolitics: Thinking and Feeling beyond the Nation*, Minneapolis: University of Minnesota Press.

Colclough, Chandler (2017), "Why I Love/Hate Nola Darling: *She's Gotta Have It* Review," *Her Campus*, December 8, <https://www.hercampus.com/school/ncat/why-i-lovehate-nola-darling-shes-gotta-have-it-review> (last accessed June 28, 2019).

Collins, Kathleen (1971), Unpublished archival material, New York: Schomburg Center for Research in Black Culture.

— (1984a), "Lecture at Howard University," Vimeo, <https://milestonefilms.com/products/losing-ground> (last accessed June 28, 2019).

— (1984b), "A Place in Time and Killer of Sheep: Two Radical Definitions of Adventure Minus Women," in *In Color: Sixty Years of Images of Minority Women in Film 1921–1981*, eds. Pearl Bowser and Ada Griffin, New York: Third World Newsreel.

— (1986), "The Brothers," in *9 Plays by Black Women*, ed. Margaret Wilkerson, New York: Penguin. Date of production 1981.

— (1991), "Losing Ground," in *Screenplays of the African American Experience*, ed. Phyllis Klotman, Bloomington: Indiana University Press.

— [1980] (2002), "In the Midnight Hour," Alexandria, VA: Alexander Street Press.

— [1980] (2015), "Commentary Track: *Cruz Brothers and Miss Malloy*," in *Losing Ground*, DVD, Harrington Park, NJ: Milestone Films.
— [1982] (2015), *Losing Ground*, DVD, Harrington Park, NJ: Milestone Films.
— (2016), *Whatever Happened to Interracial Love?: Stories*, New York: Ecco.
— [1985] (2018), *Only the Sky is Free*, Alexandria, VA: Alexander Street Press.
— (2019), *Notes from a Black Woman's Diary: Selected Works of Kathleen Collins*, ed. Nina Lorez Collins, New York: HarperCollins.
Crary, Jonathan (1999), *Suspension of Perception: Attention, Spectacle, and Modern Culture*, Cambridge, MA: MIT Press.
Cripps, Thomas (1993), "Oscar Micheaux: The Story Continues," in *Black American Cinema*, ed. Manthia Diawara, New York: Routledge, an AFI Paperback.
— (2003), "'Race Movies' as Voices of the Black Bourgeoisie: *The Scar of Shame*," in *Representing Blackness: Issues in Film and Video*, ed. Valerie Smith, New Brunswick: Rutgers University Press.
Danow, David K. (1995), *The Spirit of Carnival: Magical Realism and the Grotesque*, Lexington: University Press of Kentucky.
Davis, Zeinabu Irene (2014), "Keeping the Black in Media Production: One L.A. Rebellion Filmmaker's Notes," *Cinema Journal*, Vol. 53, No. 4: 157–61.
Derrida, Jacques (1976), *Of Grammatology*, trans. Gayatri Chakravorty Spivak, Baltimore: Johns Hopkins University Press.
Diawara, Manthia (1993), "Black American Cinema: The New Realism," in *Black American Cinema*, ed. Manthia Diawara, New York: Routledge, an AFI Paperback.
Diawara, Manthia, and Phyllis Klotman (1990), *Ganja and Hess: Vampires, Sex, and Addictions*," *Jump Cut*, No. 35: 30–6.
Donalson, Melvin (2003), *Black Directors in Hollywood*, Austin: University of Texas Press.
Doy, Gen (2000), *Black Visual Culture: Modernity and Postmodernity*, New York: I. B. Tauris.
Du Cille, Ann (1994), "The Occult of True Black Womanhood: Critical Demeanor and Black Feminist Studies," *Signs: Journal of Women in Culture and Society*, Vol. 19, No. 31: 591–629.
Eisenstein, Sergei (1949), *Film Form: Essays in Film Theory*, ed. and trans. Jay Leyda, New York: Harcourt, Brace.
Fabe, Marilyn (2018), *Closely Watched Films: An Introduction to the Art of Narrative Film Technique*, Berkeley: University of California Press.
Fischer, Lucy (2013), *Body Double: The Author Incarnate in the Cinema*, New Brunswick: Rutgers University Press.

Flinn, Caryl (1992), *Strains of Utopia: Gender, Nostalgia, and Hollywood Film Music*, Princeton: Princeton University Press.

Flory, Dan (2006), "Spike Lee and the Sympathetic Racist," "Thinking Through Cinema: Film as Philosophy," Special Issue of *The Journal of Aesthetics and Art Criticism*, Vol. 64, No. 1: 67–79.

Forster, Nicholas (2015), "Unsettling the Archive: *Tell It Like It Is* and the Constitutive Possibilities of Black Film History," *Film Quarterly*, Vol. 69, No. 1: 64–71.

Francis, Terri (2007), "Cinema on the Lower Frequencies: Black Independent Filmmaking," *Black Camera*, Vol. 22, No. 1: 19–21.

Franklin, Oliver (1980), "Kathleen Collins in Conversation with Oliver Franklin," <https://cdn.shopify.com/s/files/1/0150/7896/files/LosingGroundPK.pdf?287858186427911770> (last accessed June 28, 2019). Reprinted from 2nd National Black Films and Filmmakers Series.

— (1981), "Interview mit Kathleen Collins," *Kinemathek*, Vol. 58 (March).

Gabriel, Teshome H. (2001), "Thoughts on Nomadic Aesthetics and Black Independent Cinema: Traces of a Journey" (1991), in *Out There: Marginalization and Contemporary Cultures*, eds. Russell Ferguson, Martha Gever, Trinh T. Minh-ha, and Cornel West, Cambridge, MA: MIT Press.

Gaines, Jane (1990), "White Privilege and Looking Relations: Race and Gender in Feminist Film Theory," in *Issues in Feminist Film Criticism*, ed. Patricia Erens, Bloomington: Indiana University Press.

— (1993), "Fire and Desire: Race, Melodrama, and Oscar Micheaux," in *Black American Cinema*, ed. Manthia Diawara, New York: Routledge, an AFI Paperback.

Gates, Racquel (2017), "The Last Shall be the First: Aesthetics and Politics in Black Film and Media," *Film Quarterly*, Vol. 71, No. 2: 38–45.

Gibson, Gloria J. (2002), "Black Women's Independent Cinema," in *Experimental Cinema: The Film Reader*, eds. Wheeler Winston Dixon and Gwendolyn Audrey Foster, London: Routledge.

Gillespie, Michael (2016), *Film Blackness: American Cinema and the Idea of Black Film*, Durham, NC: Duke University Press.

Gramsci, Antonio (1971), *Selections from the Prison Notebooks of Antonio Gramsci*, ed. and trans. Quintin Hoare and Geoffrey Nowell Smith, New York: International Publishers.

Guerrero, Ed (2002), Commentary, in *BaadAsssss Cinema: A Bold Look at 70s Blaxploitation Films*, documentary, directed by Isaac Julien, New York: New Video Group.

Hachard, Tomas (2015), "'Losing Ground' Steps Forward at Lincoln Center," *National Public Radio*, Movie Reviews, February 5, <https://www.npr.org/2015/02/05/383564277/losing-ground-steps-forward-at-lincoln-center?t=1561733481050> (last accessed 28 June, 2019).

Harris, Keith (2006), *Boys, Boyz, Bois: An Ethics of Black Masculinity in Film and Popular Media*, New York: Routledge.
— (2016), "Close-up: Black Film and Black Visual Culture," *Black Camera*, Vol. 8, No. 1: 124–7.
Holland, Norman N. (n.d.), "Éric Rohmer, *Ma nuit chez Maud/My Night at Maud's* (1969)," *A Sharper Focus: Essays on Film by Norman Holland*, <http://www.asharperfocus.com/Maud.html> (last accessed June 28, 2019).
Hollinger, Karen (2012), *Feminist Film Studies*, London: Routledge.
hooks, bell (1995), *Art on My Mind: Visual Politics*, New York: The New Press.
Horak, Jan-Christopher (2015), "*Losing Ground* (1982) with Julie Dash Q&A," *UCLA Film and Television Archive*, July 31, <https://www.cinema.ucla.edu/blogs/archival-spaces/2015/07/31/losing-ground> (last accessed June 28, 2019).
Hutcheon, Linda (2003), *The Politics of Postmodernism*, 2nd ed., New York: Routledge.
Insdorf, Annette (2017), *Cinematic Overtures: How to Read Opening Scenes*, New York: Columbia University Press.
Irigaray, Luce (1985a), "Speculum," in *Speculum of the Other Woman*, trans. Gillian C. Gill, Ithaca: Cornell University Press.
— (1985b), *This Sex which is Not One*, trans. Catherine Porter with Carolyn Burke, Ithaca: Cornell University Press.
Jackson, Chuck (2018), "The Touch of the 'First' Black Cinematographer in North America: James E. Hinton, *Ganja and Hess*, and the NEA Films and the Harvard Film Archive," *Black Camera*, Vol. 10, No. 1: 67–95.
Jameson, Fredric (1986), "On Magic Realism in Film," *Critical Inquiry*, Vol. 12, No. 2: 303–11.
— (1991), *Postmodernism or the Cultural Logic of Late Capitalism*, Durham, NC: University of North Carolina Press.
Jones, Jacquie (1992), "The Accusatory Space," in *Black Popular Culture*, ed. Gina Dent, Seattle: Bay Press.
— (1993), "The Construction of Black Sexuality," in *Black American Cinema*, ed. Manthia Diawara, New York: Routledge, an AFI Paperback.
Kilpeläinen, Pekka (2012), "Mapping the Transcultural Impulse of Postcategorical Utopia: Modernity and Its Black Counterculture in James Baldwin's *Just Above My Head*," "Otherness Essays and Studies," Special Issue of *Transcultural Studies*, Vol. 3, No. 1: 1–13.
Klotman, Phyllis Rauch [1982] (2015), "Interview with Kathleen Collins," in *Losing Ground*, DVD, Harrington Park, NJ: Milestone Video.
— (ed.) (1991), *Screenplays of the African American Experience*, Bloomington: Indiana University Press.

Kristeva, Julia [1969] (1982), *Desire in Language*, ed. Leon Roudiez, trans. Tom Gora and Alice Jardine, New York: Columbia University Press.

Kurnick, David (2011), *Empty Houses: Theatrical Failure and the Novel*, Princeton: Princeton University Press.

Lopez, Ana M. (1991), "Are All Latins from Manhattan?: Hollywood, Ethnography, and Cultural Colonialism," in *Unspeakable Images: Ethnicity and the American Cinema*, ed. Lester Friedman, Urbana: University of Illinois Press.

McCabe, Janet (2004), *Feminist Film Studies: Writing the Woman into Cinema*, London: Wallflower Press.

Majumdar, Saikat (2015), *Prose of the World: Modernism and the Banality of Empire*, New York: Columbia University Press.

Manatu, Norma (2003), *African American Women and Sexuality in the Cinema*, Jefferson, NC: McFarland.

Marriot, David (2007), *Haunted Life: Visual Culture and Black Modernity*, New Brunswick: Rutgers University Press.

Mars, Louis [1946] (1977), *The Crisis of Possession in Voodoo*, Port-au-Prince: Reed, Cannon & Johnson.

Masilela, Ntongela (1993), "The Los Angeles School of Filmmakers," in *Black American Cinema*, ed. Manthia Diawara, New York: Routledge, an AFI Paperback.

Mask, Mia (ed.) (2009), *Divas on Screen: Black Women in American Film*, Urbana: University of Illinois Press.

Mast, Gerald, and Bruce F. Kawin (2011), *A Short History of the Movies*, 11th ed., Boston: Longman.

Matthews, Nadine (2017), "Visionary Filmmaker Kathleen Collins Featured at Upcoming BAM Series," *New York Amsterdam News*, March 22.

Mbembe, Achille (2017), *Critique of Black Reason*, trans. Laurent Dubois, Durham, NC: Duke University Press.

Mellier, Denis (2018), "Pléthora de doubles: saturation, épuisement, persistence à propos du cinema du double contemporain," in *Le double: littérature, arts, cinéma*, Paris: Honoré Champion Éditeur.

Mercer, Kobena (1994), *Welcome to the Jungle: New Positions in Black Cultural Studies*, New York: Routledge.

Mims, Sergio Alejandro (1990), "A New Life: Independent Black Filmmaking during the 1980s," *Black Camera*, Vol. 5, No. 1: 3–4.

Minh-ha, Trinh T. (1991), *When the Moon Waxes Red: Representation Gender and Cultural Politics*, New York: Routledge.

Nasta, Dominique (1991), *Meaning in Film: Relevant Structures in Soundtrack and Narrative*, Berne: Peter Lang.

Neal, Larry (1968), "The Black Arts Movement," *The Drama Review: TDR*, Vol. 12, No. 4: 28–39.

Nicholson, David (1988/9), "A Commitment to Writing: A Conversation with Kathleen Collins Prettyman," *Black Film Review*, Vol. 5, No. 1: 6–15.

Okiti, Tega (2016), "Ecstatic Truths," *Sight and Sound*, Vol. 26, No. 6: 36–8.

O'Malley, Hayley (2019), "Art on Her Mind: The Making of Kathleen Collins's Cinema of Interiority," *Black Camera*, Vol. 10, No. 2: 80–103.

Parkerson, Michelle (1988/9), "Remembering Kathleen Conwell Collins Prettyman," *Black Film Review*, Vol. 5, No. 1: 5.

Petrowski, Nathalie (1981), "The Cruz Brothers and Miss Malloy," *Kinemathek*, Vol. 58 (March).

Peucker, Brigitte (1995), *Incorporating Images: Film and the Rival Arts*, Princeton: Princeton University Press.

Phillips, Caryl (2005), *Dancing in the Dark*, New York: Vintage Books.

Ramanathan, Geetha (2006), *Feminist Auteurs: Reading Women's Films*, London: Wallflower Press. See in particular ch. 5, pp. 141–68.

— (2015), "Sound and Feminist Modernity in Black Women's Film Narratives," in *Feminisms*, eds. Laura Mulvey and Anna Beckman Rogers, Amsterdam: Amsterdam University Press.

Ramanathan, Geetha, and Stacey Schlau (1995), "Third World Women's Texts and the Politics of Feminist Criticism," "Third World Women's Inscriptions," eds. Geetha Ramanathan and Stacey Schlau, Special Issue of *College Literature*, Vol. 22, No. 1: 1–9.

Reed, Ishmael [1980] (2018), Jacket Notes to *Bill Gunn: Personal Problems*, New York: Kino Lorber.

Reid, Mark A. (1993), *Redefining Black Film*, Berkeley: University of California Press.

— (1997), *Postnegritude Visual and Literary Culture*, Albany: State University of New York Press.

— (2005), *Black Lenses, Black Voices: African American Film Now*, Lanham, MD: Rowman & Littlefield.

Rhinehart, Zoë (2016), "Kathleen Collins's *Losing Ground*," *Music and Literature*, April 14, <http://www.musicandliterature.org/reviews/2016/4/14/kathleen-collinss-losing-ground> (last accessed June 28, 2019).

Roh, Franz (1925), *Nach-Expressionismus: Probleme der neuesten europäischen Malerei*, Leipzig: Klinkhardt und Bierman.

Roth, Henry (1989), *The Cruz Chronicle*, New Brunswick: Rutgers University Press.

Rushton, Richard (2012), *Cinema after Deleuze*, New York: Continuum.

Ryan, Judylyn (2005), *Spirituality as Ideology in Black Women's Film and Literature*, Charlottesville: University of Virginia Press.

Sanders, Julie (2006), *Adaptation and Appropriation*, London: Routledge.

Sartre, Jean-Paul [1952] (1963), *Saint Genet: Actor and Martyr*, trans. Bernard Frechtman, New York: George Braziller.

Schjeldahl, Peter (2001), "Picasso's Lust," *The New Yorker,* July 1, <https://www.newyorker.com/magazine/2001/07/09/picassos-lust> (last accessed 28 June, 2019).

SD (n.d.), Review in *Événement.*

Shelby, Tommie, and Paul Gilroy (2008), "Cosmopolitanism, Blackness and Utopia," *Transition,* No. 98: 116–23.

Silverman, Kaja (1992), *Male Subjectivity at the Margins,* New York: Routledge.

Smith, Murray, and Thomas E. Wartenberg (eds.) (2006), *Thinking through Cinema: Film as Philosophy,* Malden, MA: Blackwell Publishing.

Sprengler, Christine (2009), *Screening Nostalgia: Populuxe Props and Technicolor Aesthetics in Contemporary American Film,* New York: Berghahn Books.

Stallings, L. H. (2011), "'Redemptive Softness': Interiority, Intellect, and Black Women's Ecstasy in Kathleen Collins's *Losing Ground,*" *Black Camera,* Vol. 2, No. 2: 47–62.

— (2015), "Kathleen Collins: Quiet Genius, Out of Time and Place," <https://cdn.shopify.com/s/files/1/0150/7896/files/LosingGroundPK.pdf?287858186427911770> (last accessed June 28, 2019).

Sterritt, David (2007), "He Cuts Heads: Spike Lee and the New York Experience," in *City That Never Sleeps: New York and the Filmic Imagination,* ed. Murray Pomerance, New Brunswick: Rutgers University Press.

Stewart, Jacqueline Najuma (2005), *Migrating to the Movies: Cinema and Black Urban Modernity,* Berkeley: University of California Press.

Streible, Dan (1993), "The Harlem Theater: Black Film Exhibition in Austin, Texas, 1920–1973," in *Black American Cinema,* ed. Manthia Diawara, New York: Routledge, an AFI Paperback.

Szaloky, Melinda (2002), "Sounding Images in Silent Film: Visual Acoustics in Murnau's *Sunrise,*" *Cinema Journal,* Vol. 41, No. 2: 109–31.

Taylor, Clyde (1995), "The Paradox of Black Independent Cinema," in *Cinemas of the Black Diaspora: Diversity, Dependence, and Oppositionality,* ed. Michael T. Martin, Detroit: Wayne State University Press.

Thompson, Robert Farris (2000), Interview on *Daughters of the Dust,* directed by Julie Dash, DVD. USA: Kino.

Walker, Alice (1983), *In Search of Our Mothers' Gardens: Womanist Prose,* San Diego: Harcourt Brace and Jovanovich.

Walkowitz, Rebecca (2006), *Cosmopolitan Style: Modernism beyond the Nation,* New York: Columbia University Press.

Wallace, Michele (1993a), "*Boyz N the Hood* and *Jungle Fever,*" in *Black Popular Culture,* ed. Gina Dent. Seattle: Bay Press.

— (1993b), "Modernism, Postmodernism, and the Problem of the Visual in Euro-American Culture," in *Aesthetics in Feminist Perspective,* eds. Hilde Hein and Carolyn Korsmeyer, Bloomington: Indiana University Press.

Webster's New Collegiate Dictionary (1981), Springfield, MA: G. & C. Merriam.

Wiegand, Daniel (2015), "'Performed Live and Talking: No Kinematograph': Amateur Performances of Tableaux Vivants and Local Film Exhibitions in Germany around 1910," in *Performing New Media, 1890–1915*, eds. Kaveh Askari, Scott Curtis, Frank Gray, Louis Pelletier, Tami Williams, and Joshua Yumibe, New Barnet: John Libbey.

Willemen, Paul (1994), "The Third Cinema Question: Notes and Reflections," in *Questions of Third Cinema*, eds. Jim Pines and Paul Willemen, London: British Film Institute.

Williams, John (1994), "Re-creating Their Media Image: Two Generations of Black Women Filmmakers," *Cineaste*, Vol. 20, No. 3: 38–41.

Wittig, Monique (1976), *The Lesbian Body*, trans. David Le Vay, New York: Avon, a Bard book.

Woll, Alan (1981), "How Hollywood Has Portrayed Hispanics," *New York Times*, March 1.

Woloch, Alex (2003), *The One vs. The Many: Minor Characters and the Space of the Protagonist in the Novel*, Princeton: Princeton University Press.

Yancy, George (1998), *African American Philosophers: 17 Conversations*, New York: Routledge.

Yancy, George (ed.) (2004), *What White Looks Like: African-American Philosophers on the Whiteness Question*, New York: Routledge.

Filmography

The Abyss, directed by Urban Gad. Denmark: Kosmorama, 1910.
The Other, directed by Max Mack. Germany: Vitascope, 1913.
The Student of Prague, directed by Stellan Rye. Germany: Deutsche Biscop, 1913.
The Birth of a Nation, directed by D. W. Griffith. USA: Epoch, 1915.
Broken Blossoms, directed by D. W. Griffith. USA: United Artists, 1919.
Within Our Gates, directed by Oscar Micheaux. USA: Micheaux Book and Film Company, 1919.
The Cabinet of Dr. Caligari, directed by Robert Wiene. Germany: Decla–Bioscop, 1920.
The Smiling Madame Beudet, directed by Germaine Dulac. France: Film d'Art/Vandal/Dulac-Aubert, 1923.
Ballet Mécanique, directed by Fernand Léger. France: Fernand Léger/Dudley Murphy, 1924.
Body and Soul, directed by Oscar Micheaux. USA: Micheaux Book and Film Company, 1925.
Berlin: Symphony of a Great City, directed by Walter Ruttmann. Germany: Fox Europa, 1927.
The Scar of Shame, directed by Frank Peregini (as Frank Perugini). USA: Philadelphia Colored Players Film Corporation, 1927.
Sunrise, directed by F. W. Murnau. USA: Fox, 1927.
The Seashell and the Clergyman, directed by Germaine Dulac. France: Germaine Dulac, 1928.
The Blue Angel, directed by Josef von Sternberg. Germany: UFA, 1930.
Dr. Jekyll and Mr. Hyde, directed by Rouben Mamoulian. USA: Paramount Pictures, 1931.
Christopher Strong, directed by Dorothy Arzner. USA: RKO, 1933.
Imitation of Life, directed by John M. Stahl. USA: Universal, 1934.
The Blood of Jesus, directed by Spencer Williams. USA, Amegro Films, 1941.
Citizen Kane, directed by Orson Welles. USA: RKO, 1941.

Bright Road, directed by Gerald Mayer. USA: MGM, 1953.
Carmen Jones, directed by Otto Preminger. USA: Otto Preminger, 1954.
Touch of Evil, directed by Orson Welles. USA: Universal International, 1958.
Breathless, directed by Jean-Luc Godard. France: SNC, 1960.
Jules and Jim, directed by François Truffaut. France: Films du Carosse/Sedif, 1962.
May Be the Last Time, directed by Larry Neal, 1969. Item number 14636, James E. Hinton Collection, Harvard Film Archive, Fine Arts Library, Harvard University.
My Night with Maud, directed by Éric Rohmer. France: Pierre Cottrell and Barbet Schroeder, 1969.
One Last Look, directed by Charles Hobson. USA: [no producer listed], 1969.
The Pirate's Fiancée, directed by Nelly Kaplan. France: Cythère Films, 1969.
Cotton Comes to Harlem, directed by Ossie Davis. USA: Samuel Goldwyn Jr., 1970.
Stock Exchange Transplant, directed by Douglas Collins. USA: [no producer listed], 1970.
Touching Ground, directed by Douglas Collins. USA: [no producer listed], 1970.
Shaft, directed by Gordon Parks. USA: MGM, 1971.
Sweet Sweetback's Baadasssss Song, directed by Melvin Van Peebles. USA: Jerry Gross and Melvin Van Peebles, 1971.
Ganja and Hess, directed by Bill Gunn. USA: Bill Schulz, 1973.
Bush Mama, directed by Haile Gerima. USA: Haile Gerima, 1974.
Mahogany, directed by Berry Gordy. USA: Motown Productions, 1975.
Killer of Sheep, directed by Charles Burnett. USA: Charles Burnett, 1977.
A Place in Time, directed by Charles Lane. USA: Charles Lane, 1977.
The Cruz Brothers and Miss Malloy, directed by Kathleen Collins. USA: CGR Productions, Eleanor Charles, and various non-profit agencies, 1980.
I Remember Harlem, directed by William Miles. USA: [no producer listed], 1981.
Will, directed by Jessie Maple. USA: [no producer listed], 1981.
Losing Ground, directed by Kathleen Collins. USA: Kathleen Collins and Ronald K. Gray, 1982.
A Question of Silence, directed by Marleen Gorris. Netherlands: Quartet Films, 1982.
Joe's Bed-Stuy Barbershop: We Cut Heads, directed by Spike Lee. USA: Spike Lee and Zimmie Shelton, 1983.
Hour of the Star, directed by Suzana Amaral. Brazil: Assunção Hernandez, 1985.
The Purple Rose of Cairo, directed by Woody Allen. USA: Robert Greenhut et al., 1985.

Vagabond, directed by Agnès Varda. USA: Ciné-Tamaris, 1985.
She's Gotta Have It, directed by Spike Lee. USA: Island Pictures, 1986.
Angel Heart, directed by Alan Parker. USA: Alan Marshall and Elliot Kastner, 1987.
Lethal Weapon, directed by Richard Donner. USA: Richard Donner and Joel Silver, 1987.
Colors, directed by Dennis Hopper. USA: Robert H. Soto, 1988.
Do the Right Thing, directed by Spike Lee. USA: A Forty Acres and a Mule Production, 1989.
Looking for Langston, directed by Isaac Julien. UK: Sankofa Film and Video, 1989.
Sidewalk Stories, directed by Charles Lane. USA: Charles Lane, 1989.
Boyz N the Hood, directed by John Singleton. USA: Steve Nicolaides, 1991.
Daughters of the Dust, directed by Julie Dash. USA: A Geechee Girls Production, 1991.
Jungle Fever, directed by Spike Lee. USA: A Forty Acres and a Mule Production, 1991.
New Jack City, directed by Mario Van Peebles. USA: Doug McHenry and George Jackson, 1991.
Straight Out of Brooklyn, directed by Matty Rich. USA: Matty Rich, 1991.
Deep Cover, directed by Bill Duke. USA: Pierre David and Henry Bean, 1992.
Juice, directed by Ernest R. Dickerson. USA: David Heyman and Neal H. Moritz, 1992.
L'Amant, directed by Jean-Jacques Annaud. France: A Renn Production, 1992.
White Men Can't Jump, directed by Ron Shelton. USA: David Lester, Don Miller, and Michele Rappaport, 1992.
Bhaji on the Beach, directed by Gurinder Chadha. UK: Nadine Marsh-Edwards, 1993.
Made in America, directed by Richard Benjamin. USA: Studio Canal and Regency Enterprises, 1993.
Watermelon Woman, directed by Cheryl Dunye. USA: Barry Swimar and Alexandra Juhasz, 1996.
Artemisia, directed by Agnès Merlet. France/Germany/Italy: Christoph Meyer-Weil and Leo Pescaralo, 1998.
Shaft, directed by John Singleton. USA: Scott Rudin and John Singleton, 2000.
Frida, directed by Julie Taymor. USA: Sarah Green, 2002.
BlacKkKlansman, directed by Spike Lee. USA: A Forty Acres and a Mule Production, 2018.
Shaft, directed by Tim Story. USA: Kenya Baris, Tim Story et al., 2019.

Index

The Abyss, 49
African American folklore, folktale, 33, 47, 77, 108
African American melodrama, 85
Albee, Edward, 142
Alexander, Elizabeth, 114
Allen, Woody, 118, 142
"Almost Music: A Cabaret Play," 141–2
Althusser, Louis, 66
Amaral, Suzana, 24
Annaud, Jean-Jacques, 24
Arzner, Dorothy, 52, 59, 135
Asante, Amma, 53
Astruc, Alexandre, 53
auteurship, 11, 51–6

Baldwin, James, 29
Barthes, Roland, Barthesian, 107
Bazin, André, 120, 124
Bhaji on the Beach, 77
Birth of a Nation, 145
black aesthetic, 40–1

Black Arts, 41
black femininity, 12
black masculinity, 12, 114, 145–8
The Blacks, 42, 142
Blaxploitation, 52
The Blue Angel, 78
Body and Soul, 105
Boyz N the Hood, 146
Breathless, 68, 102, 105
Breton, André, 117
"The Brothers," 143
Brown vs. Board of Education, 6
Burnett, Charles, 8, 18–19, 149
Bush Mama, 18, 19

Camus, Albert, 68, 118–19
capital, capitalism, 89–90
Carmen Jones, 47, 80
Carpentier, Alejo, 57
Carter, Steve, 28
Cassel, Valerie, 115
Chadha, Gurinder, 17, 53, 77
Christopher Strong, 59

Cinema of Hunger, 34
Cinema Novo, 34
Citizen Kane, 90
Coleman, Ornette, 143
cosmopolitanism, cosmopolitan, 11, 36–7, 38–40, 143
counter-cinema, 52
The Cruz Chronicle, 55–6, 58

Dancing in the Dark, 77
Dandridge, Dorothy, 47, 79–80, 122, 147
Dash, Julie, 15, 43, 53, 140
Daughters of the Dust, 140
Davis, Angela, 75
Deleuze, Gilles, 68
Deren, Maya, 47
Diawara, Manthia, 2, 5, 20, 35
Do the Right Thing, 25
Du Bois, W. E. B., 37
Dulac, Germaine, 114
Dunye, Cheryl, 53, 55
Duras, Marguerite, 24

Eisenstein, Sergei, 68, 97–8
Ellington, Duke, 143
existential, existentialism, 65, 79, 79, 109, 127, 132
Expressionism, Expressionist, 58, 133, 142

Freedom Riders, 6
French New Wave, 31
Frida, 120

Gabriel, Teshome, 19, 91, 131
Gaines, Jane, 85, 145
Gandhi, M. K., 144
Ganja and Hess, 16, 17, 20–1, 22, 57
Genet, Jean, 33, 42, 66, 70, 75, 119, 142
Gerima, Haile, 18
Godard, Jean Luc, 68, 102, 105
Gorris, Marleen, 114
Gramsci, Antonio 60, 66
Griffith, D. W., 2, 51, 117, 144
Gunn, Bill, 17, 21, 29, 30, 54, 150

Hansberry, Lorraine, 37–8
Harper, Frances, 81
Hays Code, 3, 4, 144
Head, Bessie, 37
Hegelian dialectic, 4, 33
Hepburn, Katherine, 59
Hitchcock, Alfred, 11, 51, 81
Hobson, Charles, 28
Horne, Lena, 76
Hudson River School, 17
Hurston, Zora Neale, 22–3, 41, 46
Hutcheon, Linda, 94

imperfect cinema, 18
"In the Midnight Hour," 142–3
Iola Leroy, 81
Irigaray, Luce, 25, 33, 46, 66, 79, 136

Jackson, Samuel, 148
Jameson, Fredric, 87, 89–91, 93–4, 97
Jim Crow, 6, 7
Joe's Bed-Stuy Barbershop, 56
Jones, Duane, 30
Jones, Jacquie, 145
Josh Lawrence Quintet, 127
Joyce, James, 97–8
Jules and Jim, 102–3, 105
Jungle Fever, 146

Kandinsky, Vassily, 127
Kaplan, Nelly, 33
Killer of Sheep, 18, 19, 22, 57
King Jr., M. L. K., 7, 144
Kokoschka, Oskar, 133, 136
Kristeva, Julia, Kristevan, 94, 144

LA Independents, 4, 11, 14, 17, 18, 31, 52
Lane, Charles, 14
Larkin, Alile Sharon, 4
Larsen, Nella, 148
Lawrence, D. H., Laurentian, 133
Lee, Spike, 3, 4, 8, 14, 22, 54, 56, 146
Léger, Fernand, 90
"Lila," 136–8
Lukács, Georg, Lukácsian, 19, 144

McCormack, Pearl, 122–3, 147
McCrae, Carmen, 143

Márquez, Gabriel García, 42, 58, 83
Mars, Louis, 21, 33, 46, 106–7, 109
Merleau-Ponty, Maurice, 126
Merlet, Agnès, 57
Meyers, Nancy, 114
Micheaux, Oscar, 13, 85–6, 105, 147, 148
Minard, Michael, 141
minority, minorities, 8, 12, 14, 38, 42, 111, 132, 150
modern, modernity, 86–7, 89, 95, 127, 142, 151
modernism, modernist, modernist aesthetics, 8, 12, 14, 37–8, 49, 87, 90, 93, 97–8, 101, 108, 110–11, 116, 119, 125–6, 128, 136, 137, 151
  black modernism, 41
  engaged modernism, 60
Moynihan Report, 146
Murnau, F. W., 121, 130
My Night with Maud, 32, 68, 84–5, 104

nationalism, nationalist, 37, 100–1, 146
Neue Sachlichkeit, 87
Nielsen, Asta, 49
nostalgia, 89–90, 93–5, 97–8

O'Day, Anita, 143
One Hundred Years of Solitude, 58–9, 83, 87, 89
One Last Look, 28–9

Personal Problems, 29–30
Peucker, Brigitte, 121
Phillips, Caryl, 77
Pirandello, Luigi, 63
A Place in Time, 22, 27–8
postmodern, 118
post-structuralist discourse, 36, 53

Quicksand, 148

Race Films, 13, 147
realism, realist, 26, 29, 35, 38, 40, 60, 61, 84, 98–100, 110, 114, 118, 123, 144, 150
  magical realism, 11, 38, 58, 86–9, 91–3, 95, 97, 99–100, 151
  marvelous realism, 86–7, 90–1, 93–4, 97, 99–100, 134, 151
  mythical realism, 88, 151
  New Realism, 19, 100, 146
  surrealism, surrealist, 58, 87, 117, 133, 136
Reed, Ishmael, 29
Rilke, Rainer Maria, 134
Rocha, Glauber, 19, 34
Roh, Franz, 87

Rohmer, Éric, 31, 32, 42, 68, 84–6, 102, 104–5
romance, romance, 18, 20, 27, 101–2, 105, 141
romantic, Romantic, Romanticism, 17, 98, 102–3, 105–6, 113–16, 130, 141
Roth, Henry, 8, 29, 55–6, 58, 60–1, 83
Roundtree, Richard, 148
Ruttman, Walter, 27

Sartre, Jean-Paul, 33, 42, 65, 70, 79, 118–20
The Scar of Shame, 80, 122–3, 147
Scott, Seret, 20, 30, 81
The Seashell and the Clergyman, 136
Shaft, 148
She's Gotta Have It, 22
Sidewalk Stories, 27–8
silent cinema, Silent era, 13, 27, 52, 81, 97–8, 99n, 117, 121–2, 147
Singleton, John, 146
"Stepping Back," 144–5
subaltern discourse, subaltern people, 36
"A Summer Diary," 139–41
Sweet Sweetback's Baadasssss Song, 52, 100, 148
synesthesia, synesthetic, 126–7

Taymor, Julie, 57, 120
Third Cinema, 18

Touch of Evil, 120
Truffaut, François, 11, 51, 102, 105
Tucker, Lorenzo, 64

universal, universalism, universalist, universality, universalize, 11, 35, 37–8, 40–4, 45, 47, 50, 53, 54, 55, 56, 69, 70, 84–5, 86, 90, 98, 100–2, 119, 123, 132, 139, 142, 143, 146, 150

Van Peebles, Mario, 23
Van Peebles, Melvin, 52, 100, 148
Varda, Agnès, 31–2
vaudun, 21, 46, 106–9, 111, 131, 134

Von Sternberg, Josef, 78
Von Trotta, Margarethe, 52

Walker, Alice, 55
Wallace, Michele, 2, 23, 146
Watermelon Woman, 55
Welles, Orson, 120
Who's Afraid of Virginia Woolf?, 142
Wiene, Robert, 117
Williams, Bert, 77
Williams, Spencer, 20
Within Our Gates, 85, 105
Wittig, Monique, 25
"Women, Sisters, and Friends," 132–4, 140
Woolf, Virginia, 55
world literature, 33, 38, 86, 132

EU representative:
Easy Access System Europe
Mustamäe tee 50, 10621 Tallinn, Estonia
Gpsr.requests@easproject.com

www.ingramcontent.com/pod-product-compliance
Lightning Source LLC
Chambersburg PA
CBHW071205160426
43196CB00011B/2201